Careers in Focus

AVIATION

SECOND EDITION

Ferguson

An imprint of Infobase Publishing

Careers in Focus: Aviation, Second Edition

Copyright © 2011 by Infobase Publishing

Ferguson
An imprint of Infobase Publishing
132 West 31st Street
New York NY 10001

Library of Congress Cataloging-in-Publication Data
Careers in focus. Aviation. — 2nd ed.
    p. cm.
    Includes bibliographical references and index.
    ISBN-13: 978-0-8160-8023-6 (hardcover: alk. paper)
    ISBN-10: 0-8160-8023-2 (hardcover: alk. paper) 1. Aeronautics—Vocational guidances. I. Title: Aviation. II. Title: Ferguson's careers in focus. Aviation.

TL561.C376 2010
387.7023—dc22

Ferguson books are available at special discounts when purchased in bulk quantities for businesses, associations, institutions, or sales promotions. Please call our Special Sales Department in New York at (212) 967-8800 or (800) 322-8755.

You can find Ferguson on the World Wide Web at
http://www.infobasepublishing.com

Text design by David Strelecky
Composition by Lina Farinella
Cover printed by Art Print, Taylor, PA
Book printed and bound by Maple Press, York, PA
Date printed: November 2010
Printed in the United States of America

10 9 8 7 6 5 4 3 2 1

Table of Contents

Introduction

Careers in Focus: Aviation describes a variety of careers in the aviation industry, at airports, flight schools, factories, customer service centers, travel agencies, shipping companies, and in military settings. These careers are as diverse in nature as they are in their earnings and educational requirements. Earnings range from minimum wage for entry-level airport service workers to $150,000 or more for pilots, air traffic controllers, and some airport security workers. A few of these careers—such as airport food service worker and skycap—require little formal education, but are excellent starting points for a career in the industry. Other jobs, many of which are technical in nature, require some postsecondary training or an associate's degree. Examples of these careers include aeronautical and aerospace technicians, aircraft mechanics, and avionics technicians. The most advanced positions require either a minimum of a bachelor's degree (aerospace engineers, air traffic controllers, and avionics engineers) or a combination of postsecondary training and flight certification (flight instructors and pilots) from the Federal Aviation Administration.

The U.S. Department of Labor's *Career Guide to Industries* predicts that employment in the aerospace product and parts manufacturing industry will experience little or no change through 2018. The air transportation industry is projected to grow by 7 percent through 2018—or 4 percent less than the average for all industries. The events of September 11, 2001, and the economic recession have had a major impact on both the aerospace products and parts manufacturing industry and the air transportation industry. Layoffs, mergers, and bankruptcies have hit both industries hard as the number of air passengers decreased.

The U.S. Department of Labor (DOL) predicts that the employment decline in the manufacturing segment of the aviation industry will be partially offset by a growing demand for military aircraft and military aerospace equipment, which will be used in defensive and offensive operations in the United States and abroad.

Our growing population, a gradually improving economy, and increases in international business and shipping should help the airline industry bounce back to pre-9/11 levels and provide good opportunities for workers in this field.

The articles in *Careers in Focus: Aviation* appear in Ferguson's *Encyclopedia of Careers and Vocational Guidance,* but have been updated and revised with the latest information from the DOL, professional organizations, and other sources.

The following paragraphs detail the sections and features that appear in the book.

The **Quick Facts** section provides a brief summary of the career including recommended school subjects, personal skills, work environment, minimum educational requirements, salary ranges, certification or licensing requirements, and employment outlook. This section also provides acronyms and identification numbers for the following government classification indexes: the Dictionary of Occupational Titles (DOT), the Guide for Occupational Exploration (GOE), the National Occupational Classification (NOC) Index, and the Occupational Information Network (O*NET)-Standard Occupational Classification System (SOC) index. The DOT, GOE, and O*NET-SOC indexes have been created by the U.S. government; the NOC index is Canada's career classification system. Readers can use the identification numbers listed in the Quick Facts section to access further information about a career. Print editions of the DOT (*Dictionary of Occupational Titles*. Indianapolis, Ind.: JIST Works, 1991) and GOE (*Guide for Occupational Exploration*. Indianapolis, Ind.: JIST Works, 2001) are available at libraries. Electronic versions of the NOC (http://www23.hrdc-drhc.gc.ca) and O*NET-SOC (http://online.onetcenter.org) are available on the Internet. When no DOT, GOE, NOC, or O*NET-SOC numbers are listed, this means that the DOL or Human Resources and Skills Development Canada have not created a numerical designation for this career. In this instance, you will see the acronym "N/A," or not available.

The **Overview** section is a brief introductory description of the duties and responsibilities involved in this career. Oftentimes, a career may have a variety of job titles. When this is the case, alternative career titles are presented. Employment statistics are also provided, when available. The **History** section describes the history of the particular job as it relates to the overall development of its industry or field. **The Job** describes the primary and secondary duties of the job. **Requirements** discusses high school and postsecondary education and training requirements, any certification or licensing that is necessary, and other personal requirements for success in the job. **Exploring** offers suggestions on how to gain experience in or knowledge of the particular job before making a firm educational and financial commitment. The focus is on what can be done while still in high school (or in the early years of college) to gain a better understanding of the job. The **Employers** section gives an overview of typical places of employment for the job. **Starting**

Out discusses the best ways to land that first job, be it through the college career services office, newspaper ads, Internet employment sites, or personal contact. The **Advancement** section describes what kind of career path to expect from the job and how to get there. **Earnings** lists salary ranges and describes the typical fringe benefits. The **Work Environment** section describes the typical surroundings and conditions of employment—whether indoors or outdoors, noisy or quiet, social or independent. Also discussed are typical hours worked, any seasonal fluctuations, and the stresses and strains of the job. The **Outlook** section summarizes the job in terms of the general economy and industry projections. For the most part, Outlook information is obtained from the U.S. Bureau of Labor Statistics and is supplemented by information gathered from professional associations. Job growth terms follow those used in the *Occupational Outlook Handbook*. Growth described as "much faster than the average" means an increase of 21 percent or more. Growth described as "faster than the average" means an increase of 14 to 20 percent. Growth described as "about as fast as the average" means an increase of 7 to 13 percent. Growth described as "more slowly than the average" means an increase of 3 to 6 percent. "Little or no change" means a decrease of 2 percent to an increase of 2 percent. "Decline" means a decrease of 3 percent or more. Each article ends with **For More Information**, which lists organizations that provide information on training, education, internships, scholarships, and job placement.

Careers in Focus: Aviation also includes photos, informative sidebars, and interviews with professionals in the field.

If you enjoy traveling by airplane, going to airports, meeting people from all over the world, or have a knack for mechanics or mathematics, there may be an exciting career in aviation waiting for you. Read about the careers in this varied field, and be sure to contact the organizations listed at the end of each article for more information.

Aeronautical and Aerospace Technicians

OVERVIEW

Aeronautical and aerospace technicians design, construct, test, operate, and maintain the basic structures of aircraft and spacecraft, as well as propulsion and control systems. They work with scientists and engineers. Many aeronautical and aerospace technicians assist engineers in preparing equipment drawings, diagrams, blueprints, computer-aided designs, and scale models. They collect information, make computations, and perform laboratory tests. Their duties may include working on various projects involving aerodynamics, structural design, flight-test evaluation, or propulsion problems. Other technicians estimate the cost of materials and labor required to manufacture the product, serve as manufacturers' field service technicians, and write technical materials.

HISTORY

Both aeronautical engineering and the aerospace industry had their births in the early 20th century. The very earliest machine-powered and heavier-than-air aircraft, such as the first one flown by Wilbur and Orville Wright in 1903, were crudely constructed and often the result of costly and dangerous trial-and-error experimentation.

As government and industry took an interest in the possible applications of this new invention, however, our knowledge of aircraft and the entire industry became more sophisticated. By 1908, for instance,

QUICK FACTS

School Subjects
Mathematics
Physics
Technical/shop

Personal Skills
Mechanical/manipulative
Technical/scientific

Work Environment
Primarily indoors
Primarily one location

Minimum Education Level
Associate's degree

Salary Range
$34,220 to $55,040 to $80,980+

Certification or Licensing
Required for certain positions

Outlook
Little or no change

DOT
002

GOE
02.08.04

NOC
2232

O*NET-SOC
17-3021.00, 49-2091.00, 49-3011.00

the Wright brothers had received their first government military contract, and by 1909, the industry had expanded to include additional airplane producers, such as Glenn Curtiss in the United States and several others in France.

Aeronautical engineering and the aerospace industry have been radically transformed since those early days, mostly because of the demands of two world wars and the tremendous increases in scientific knowledge that have taken place during this century. Aviation and aerospace developments continued after the end of World War II. The factories and workers that built planes to support the war were in place and the industry took off, with the jet engine, rocket propulsion, supersonic flight, and manned voyages outside the earth's atmosphere among the major developments. As the industry evolved, aeronautical and aerospace engineers found themselves taking on increasingly larger projects and were more in need of trained and knowledgeable assistants to help them. Throughout the years, these assistants have been known as *engineering aides,* as *engineering associates,* and, most recently, as *aerospace technicians and technologists.* Their main task today is to take on assignments that require technical skills but do not necessarily require the scientist's or engineer's special training and education.

THE JOB

There are no clear-cut definitions of "aeronautical technology" and "aerospace technology"; in fact, many employers use the terms interchangeably. This lack of a clear distinction also occurs in education, where many schools and institutes offer similar courses under a variety of titles: aeronautical, aviation, or aerospace technology. In general, however, the term "aerospace industry" refers to manufacturers of all kinds of flying vehicles: from piston and jet-powered aircraft that fly inside the earth's atmosphere, to rockets, missiles, satellites, probes, and all kinds of manned and unmanned spacecraft that operate outside the earth's atmosphere. The term *aeronautics* is often used within the aerospace industry to refer specifically to mechanical flight inside the earth's atmosphere, especially to the design and manufacture of commercial passenger and freight aircraft, private planes, and helicopters.

The difference between technicians and technologists generally refers to their level of education. Technicians generally hold associate's degrees, while technologists hold bachelor's degrees in aeronautical technology.

Whether they work for a private company working on commercial aircraft or for the federal government, aerospace technicians work side by side with engineers and scientists in all major phases of the design, production, and operation of aircraft and spacecraft technology. The aerospace technician position includes collecting and recording data; operating test equipment such as wind tunnels and flight simulators devising tests to ensure quality control; modifying mathematical procedures to fit specific problems; laying out experimental circuits to test scientific theories; and evaluating experimental data for practical applications.

The following paragraphs describe jobs held by aerospace technicians; some may be used in other industries as well. Fuller descriptions of the work of some of these titles are also provided in the following paragraphs.

Aerospace physiological technicians operate devices used to train pilots and astronauts. These devices include pressure suits, pressure chambers, and ejection seats that simulate flying conditions. These technicians also operate other kinds of flight training equipment such as tow reels, radio equipment, and meteorological devices. They interview trainees about their medical histories, which helps detect evidence of conditions that would disqualify pilots or astronauts from further training.

Aircraft launch and recovery technicians work on aircraft carriers to operate, adjust, and repair launching and recovery equipment such as catapults, barricades, and arresting nets. They disassemble the launch and recovery equipment, replace defective parts, and keep track of all maintenance activities.

Avionics technicians inspect, test, adjust, and repair the electronic components of aircraft communications, navigation, and flight-control systems and also operate, install, troubleshoot, and repair electronic testing equipment.

Computer technicians assist mathematicians and subject specialists in checking and refining computations and systems, such as those required for predicting and determining orbits of spacecraft.

Drafting and design technicians convert the aeronautical engineer's specifications and rough sketches of aeronautical and aerospace equipment, such as electrical and mechanical devices, into accurate drawings that are used by skilled craft workers to make parts for aircraft and spacecraft.

Engineering technicians assist with review and analysis of postflight data, structural failure, and other factors that cause failure in flight vehicles.

Industrial engineering technicians assist engineers in preparing layouts of machinery and equipment, work-flow plans, time-and-motion studies, and statistical studies and analyses of production costs to produce the most efficient use of personnel, materials, and machines.

Instrumentation technicians test, install, and maintain electronic, hydraulic, pneumatic, and optical instruments. These are used in aircraft systems and components in manufacturing as well as research and development. One important responsibility is to maintain their assigned research instruments. As a part of this maintenance, they test the instruments, take readings and calibration curves, and calculate correction factors for the instruments.

Liaison technicians check on the production of aircraft and spacecraft as they are being built for conformance to specifications, keeping engineers informed as the manufacturing progresses, and they investigate any engineering production problems that arise.

Mathematical technicians assist mathematicians, engineers, and scientists by performing computations involving the use of advanced mathematics.

Mechanical technicians use metalworking machines to assist in the manufacture of one-of-a-kind parts. They also assist in rocket-fin alignment, payload mating, weight and center-of-gravity measurements, and launch-tower erection.

Target aircraft technicians repair and maintain pilotless target aircraft. They assemble, repair, or replace aircraft parts such as cowlings, wings, and propeller assemblies and test aircraft engine operation.

Workers at a manufacturing plant assemble a PW500 engine for a Cessna Citation. (*Paul Chiasson, AP Photo/Canadian Press*)

Did You Know?

- Approximately 630,000 people were employed in the aeronautical and aerospace industries in 2007; women held approximately 15 to 20 percent of these jobs.
- There are approximately 2,900 establishments in the aerospace industry.
- The states of Washington and California offer the most aeronautical and aerospace jobs. Other states that offer strong employment opportunities include Kansas, Texas, Connecticut, and Arizona.
- In 2006, employees in aeronautical and aerospace industries worked an average of 43.8 hours a week—slightly higher than the average for all workers.
- In 2006, 21 percent of aeronautical and aerospace workers were union members—a percentage that is 8 percent higher than the national average for all private industry occupations.

Sources: U.S. Department of Labor, Aerospace Industries Association

REQUIREMENTS

High School

A strong science and mathematics background is essential for entry into this field. High school courses that will be useful in preparing you for college-level study include algebra, trigonometry, physics, and chemistry. In addition to math and science, courses in social studies, economics, history, blueprint reading, drafting, and industrial and machine shop practice will provide a valuable background for a career in aerospace technology. Computer classes are also important. English, speech, and courses in the preparation of test reports and technical writing are extremely helpful to develop communication ability.

Postsecondary Training

There are a variety of training possibilities for potential aerospace technicians: two-, three-, or four-year programs at colleges or universities, junior or community colleges, technical institutes, vocational-technical schools, industry on-the-job training, or work-study programs in the military. Graduates from a two- or three-year program usually earn an associate's degree in engineering or science. Graduates from a four-year program earn a bachelor's degree in engineering or science; in addition, several colleges offer four-year degree programs in aeronautical technology. There are also many technical training schools, particularly in areas where the aerospace industry is most active, that offer training in aeronautical technology. However, many employers require graduates of such programs to complete a period of on-the-job training before they are granted full technician status. When selecting a school to attend, check the listings of such agencies as the Accreditation Board for Engineering and Technology and the regional accrediting associations for engineering colleges. Most employers prefer graduates of an accredited school.

In general, post-high school programs strengthen the student's background in science and mathematics, including pretechnical training. Beyond that, an interdisciplinary curriculum is more helpful than one that specializes in a narrow field. Other courses, which are basic to the work of the aeronautical scientist and engineer, should be part of a balanced program. These include basic physics, nuclear theory, chemistry, mechanics, and computers, including data-processing equipment and procedures.

Certification or Licensing

Only a few aerospace technician positions require licensing or certification; however, certificates issued by professional organizations do enhance the status of qualified engineering technicians. Certification is usually required of those working with nuclear-powered engines or testing radioactive sources, for those working on aircraft in some test programs, and in some safety-related positions. Technicians and technologists working in areas related to national defense, and especially those employed by government agencies, are usually required to carry security clearances.

Other Requirements

Aeronautical and aerospace technicians must have basic engineering skills. They should enjoy and be proficient in mathematics and the physical sciences and be able to visualize size, form, and function. The Aerospace Industries Association of America advises that today's aerospace production worker must be strong in the basics of manufacturing, have a knowledge of statistics and have the ability to work with computers.

EXPLORING

Visiting an aerospace research or manufacturing facility is one of the best ways to learn more about this field. Because there are many such facilities connected with the aerospace industry throughout the

United States, there is sure to be one in nearly every area. The reference department of your local library can help you locate the nearest facility.

Finding part-time or summer employment at such a facility is, of course, one of the best ways to gain experience or learn more about the field. Such jobs aren't available for all students interested in the field, but you can still find part-time work that will give you practical experience, such as in a local machine shop or factory.

You should not overlook the educational benefits of visiting local museums of science and technology or aircraft museums or displays. The National Air and Space Museum (http://www.nasm.si.edu) at the Smithsonian Institution in Washington, D.C., is one of the most comprehensive museums dedicated to aerospace. Some air force bases or naval air stations also offer tours to groups of interested students. The tours may be arranged by your teacher or career guidance counselor.

The Junior Engineering Technical Society (JETS) provides students a chance to explore career opportunities in engineering and technology, enter academic competitions, and design model structures. JETS administers a competition that allows high school students to use their technology skills. The Tests of Engineering, Aptitude, Mathematics, and Science (http://www.jets.org/teams) is an engineering problem competition. If your school doesn't have a JETS chapter, check with other schools in your area; sometimes smaller schools can form cooperatives to offer such programs.

If you are a high school student with an interest in aerospace, you can become a student member of the American Institute of Aeronautics and Astronautics. Members receive a magazine, networking opportunities, and discounts on institute products, programs, and services.

EMPLOYERS

Aeronautical and aerospace technicians and technologists are principally employed by government agencies, commercial airlines, educational institutions, and aerospace manufacturing companies. Most technicians employed by manufacturing companies engage in research, development, and design; the remainder work in production, sales, engineering, installation and maintenance, and other related fields. Those employed by government and educational institutions are normally assigned to do research and specific problem-solving tasks. Airlines employ technicians to supervise maintenance operations and the development of procedures for new equipment.

STARTING OUT

The best way for students to obtain an aeronautical or aerospace technician's job is through their college or university's career services office. Many manufacturers maintain recruiting relationships with schools in their area. Jobs may also be obtained through state employment offices, newspaper and magazine advertisements, applications for government employment, online listings, and industry work-study programs offered by many aircraft companies.

ADVANCEMENT

Aeronautical and aerospace technicians continue to learn on the job. As they gain experience in the specialized areas, employers turn to them as experts who can solve problems, create new techniques, devise new designs, or develop practice from theory.

Most advancement involves taking on additional responsibilities. For example, with experience, a technician may take on supervisory responsibilities, overseeing several trainees, assistant technicians, or others. Such a technician may also be assigned independent responsibility, especially on some tasks usually assigned to an engineer. Technicians who have outgoing personalities and a good working knowledge of their company's equipment may become company sales or technical representatives. Technicians seeking further advancement are advised to continue their education. With additional formal education, a technician may become an aeronautical or aerospace engineer.

EARNINGS

Aerospace technology is a broad field, so earnings vary depending on a technician's specialty, educational preparation, and work experience. In 2008, the median annual earnings for aerospace technicians were $55,040. Salaries ranged from less than $34,380 to more than $80,980. Avionics technicians earned salaries that ranged from $34,220 to $64,200 or more in 2008.

Benefits depend on employers but usually include paid vacations and holidays, sick pay, health insurance, and a retirement plan. Many companies offer some form of tuition reimbursement for further education. Some offer cooperative programs with local schools, combining classroom training with practical paid experience.

WORK ENVIRONMENT

The aerospace industry, with its strong emphasis on quality and safety, is a very safe place to work. Special procedures and equipment make otherwise hazardous jobs extremely safe. The range of work covered means that the technicians can work in small teams in specialized research laboratories or in test areas that are large and hospital-clean.

Aerospace technicians are at the launch pad, involved in fueling and checkout procedures, and back in the blockhouse sitting at an electronic console. They work in large test facilities or in specialized shops, designing and fabricating equipment. They travel to test sites or tracking stations to construct facilities or troubleshoot systems. Working conditions vary with the assignment, but the work climate is always challenging, and coworkers are well-trained, competent people.

Aeronautical technicians may perform inside activities involving confined detail work, they may work outside, or they may combine both situations. Aeronautical and aerospace technicians work in many situations: alone, in small teams, or in large groups. Commonly, technicians participate in team projects, which are coordinated efforts of scientists, engineers, and technicians working on specific assignments. They concentrate on the practical aspects of the project and must get along well with and interact cooperatively with the scientists responsible for the theoretical aspects of the project.

Aerospace technicians must be able to perform under deadline pressure, meet strict requirements and rigid specifications, and deal with potentially hazardous situations. They must be willing and flexible enough to acquire new knowledge and techniques to adjust to the rapidly changing technology. In addition, technicians need persistence and tenacity, especially when engaged in experimental and research tasks. They must be responsible, reliable, and willing to accept greater responsibility.

Aerospace technology is never far from the public's attention, and aeronautical technicians have the additional satisfaction of knowing that they are viewed as being engaged in vital and fascinating work.

OUTLOOK

The *Career Guide to Industries* predicts that the aerospace product and parts manufacturing segment of the civilian aerospace industry is expected to grow by less than 2 percent (little or no change for all occupations) through 2018. Orders for commercial aircraft declined in the early 2000s, but have been slowly rebounding since 2004. Employment in the military aircraft sector is expected to be better during this same time period as a result of our nation's need for more military aircraft, aerospace equipment, and related materials.

The U.S. Department of Labor predicts that employment in the aerospace industry is also expected to experience little or no change compared to all occupations through 2018 due to more efficient production methods, a reduction of orders for new aircraft and related technology, and outsourcing of jobs in the industry. However, prospects for aircraft mechanics and avionics service technicians will remain good since, though industry conditions have created a large pool of un- or under-employed technicians, many will retire or seek employment in other industries.

Many manufacturers in the aerospace industry have responded to the decline in orders by broadening their production to include other areas of technology. The Aerospace Industries Association predicts aerospace companies will be looking for qualified technicians in fields such as laser optics, mission operations, hazardous materials procedures, production planning, materials testing, computer-aided design, and robotic operations and programming.

FOR MORE INFORMATION

For a list of accredited technology programs, contact
Accreditation Board for Engineering and Technology Inc.
111 Market Place, Suite 1050
Baltimore, MD 21202-4012
Tel: 410-347-7700
http://www.abet.org

Contact the AIA for publications with information on aerospace technologies, careers, and space.
Aerospace Industries Association (AIA)
1000 Wilson Boulevard, Suite 1700
Arlington, VA 22209-3928
Tel: 703-358-1000
http://www.aia-aerospace.org

For career information and details on membership for high school students, contact
American Institute of Aeronautics and Astronautics
1801 Alexander Bell Drive, Suite 500
Reston, VA 20191-4344
Tel: 800-639-2422
http://www.aiaa.org

For information on educational programs and to purchase a copy of Engineering: Go For It, *contact*
American Society for Engineering Education
1818 N Street, NW, Suite 600
Washington, DC 20036-2479
Tel: 202-331-3500
http://www.asee.org

For career and scholarship information, contact
General Aviation Manufacturers Association
1400 K Street, NW, Suite 801
Washington, DC 20005-2485
Tel: 202-393-1500
http://www.gama.aero

JETS has career information and offers high school students the opportunity to "try on" engineering through a number of programs and competitions. For more information, contact
Junior Engineering Technical Society Inc. (JETS)
1420 King Street, Suite 405
Alexandria, VA 22314-2750
Tel: 703-548-5387
E-mail: info@jets.org
http://www.jets.org

SEDS is an international organization of high school and college students dedicated to promoting interest in space. Its U.S. national headquarters are located at the Massachusetts Institute of Technology.
Students for the Exploration and Development of Space (SEDS)
MIT Room W20-445
77 Massachusetts Avenue
Cambridge, MA 02139-4307
E-mail: outreach@seds.org
http://www.seds.org

For more information on career choices and schools in Canada, contact
Aerospace Industries Association of Canada
60 Queen Street, Suite 1200
Ottawa, ON K1P 5Y7 Canada
Tel: 613-232-4297
E-mail: info@aiac.ca
http://www.aiac.ca

Aerospace Engineers

QUICK FACTS

School Subjects
Mathematics
Physics

Personal Skills
Mechanical/manipulative
Technical/scientific

Work Environment
Primarily indoors
One location with some travel

Minimum Education Level
Bachelor's degree

Salary Range
$53,408 to $92,520 to
$134,570+

Certification or Licensing
Required

Outlook
About as fast as the average

DOT
002

GOE
02.07.04

NOC
2146

O*NET-SOC
17-2011.00

OVERVIEW

Aerospace engineering encompasses the fields of aeronautical (aircraft) and astronautical (spacecraft) engineering. *Aerospace engineers* work in teams to design, build, and test machines that fly within the earth's atmosphere and beyond. Although aerospace science is a very specialized discipline, it is also considered one of the most diverse. This field of engineering draws from such subjects as physics, mathematics, earth science, aerodynamics, and biology. Some aerospace engineers specialize in designing one complete machine, perhaps a commercial aircraft, whereas others focus on separate components such as for missile guidance systems. There are approximately 71,600 aerospace engineers working in the United States.

HISTORY

The roots of aerospace engineering can be traced as far back as when people first dreamed of being able to fly. Thousands of years ago, the Chinese developed kites and later experimented with gunpowder as a source of propulsion. In the 15th century, Renaissance artist and inventor Leonardo da Vinci created drawings of two devices that were designed to fly. One, the ornithopter, was supposed to fly the way birds do, by flapping its wings; the other was designed as a rotating screw, closer in form to today's helicopter.

In 1783, Joseph and Jacques Montgolfier of France designed the first hot-air balloon that could be used for manned flight. In 1799, an English baron, Sir George Cayley, designed an aircraft that was one of the first not to be considered "lighter than air," as balloons were. He developed a fixed-wing structure that led to his creation of the first glider in 1849. Much experimentation was performed in gliders and the science of aerodynamics through the late 1800s. In 1903, the first mechanically powered and controlled flight was completed in a craft designed by Orville and Wilbur Wright. The big boost in airplane development occurred during World War I. In the early years of the war, aeronautical engineering encompassed a variety of engineering skills applied toward the development of flying machines. Civil engineering principles were used in structural design, while early airplane engines were devised by automobile engineers. Aerodynamic design itself was primarily empirical, with many answers coming from liquid flow concepts established in marine engineering.

The evolution of the airplane continued during both world wars, with steady technological developments in materials science, propulsion, avionics, and stability and control. Airplanes became larger and faster. Airplanes are commonplace today, but commercial flight became a frequent mode of transportation only as recently as the 1960s and 1970s.

Robert Goddard developed and flew the first liquid-propelled rocket in 1926. The technology behind liquid propulsion continued to evolve, and the first U.S. liquid rocket engine was tested in 1938. More sophisticated rockets were eventually created to enable aircraft to be launched into space. The world's first artificial satellite, *Sputnik I,* was launched by the Soviets in 1957. In 1961, President John F. Kennedy urged the United States to be the first country to put a man on the moon; on July 20, 1969, astronauts Neil Armstrong and Edwin Aldrin, Jr., accomplished that goal.

Today, aerospace engineers design spacecraft that explore beyond the earth's atmosphere. They create missiles and military aircraft of many types, such as fighters, bombers, observers, and transports. Today's engineers go beyond the dreams of merely learning to fly. For example, in 1998, the United States and 15 other countries began a series of joint missions into space to assemble a planned International Space Station. On the ground, space professionals, including aerospace engineers, have played a vital role in developing equipment that is used on the station.

THE JOB

Although the creation of aircraft and spacecraft involves professionals from many branches of engineering (e.g., materials, electrical, and mechanical), aerospace engineers in particular are responsible for the total design of the craft, including its shape, performance, propulsion, and guidance control system. In the field of aerospace engineering, professional responsibilities vary widely depending on the specific job description. Aeronautical engineers work specifically with aircraft systems, and astronautical engineers specialize in spacecraft systems.

Throughout their education and training, aerospace engineers thoroughly learn the complexities involved in how materials and structures perform under tremendous stress. In general, they are called upon to apply their knowledge of the following subjects: propulsion, aerodynamics, thermodynamics, fluid mechanics, flight mechanics, and structural analysis. Less technically scientific issues must also often be dealt with, such as cost analysis, reliability studies, maintainability, operations research, marketing, and management.

There are many professional titles given to certain aerospace engineers. *Analytical engineers* use engineering and mathematical theory to solve questions that arise during the design phase. Stress analysts determine how the weight and loads of structures behave under a variety of conditions. This analysis is performed with computers and complex formulas.

Computational fluid dynamic (CFD) engineers use sophisticated high-speed computers to develop models used in the study of fluid dynamics. Using simulated systems, they determine how elements flow around objects; simulation saves time and money and eliminates risks involved with actual testing. As computers become more complex, so do the tasks of the CFD engineer.

Design aerospace engineers draw from the expertise of many other specialists. They devise the overall structure of components and entire crafts, meeting the specifications developed by those more specialized in aerodynamics, astrodynamics, and structural engineering. Design engineers use computer-aided design programs for many of their tasks. *Manufacturing aerospace engineers* develop the plans for producing the complex components that make up aircraft and spacecraft. They work with the designers to ensure that the plans are economically feasible and will produce efficient, effective components.

Materials aerospace engineers determine the suitability of the various materials that are used to produce aerospace vehicles. Aircraft and spacecraft require the appropriate tensile strength, density, and rigidity for the particular environments they are subjected to. Determining how materials such as steel, glass, and even chemical compounds react to temperature and stress is an important part of the materials engineer's responsibilities.

Quality control is a task that *quality control aerospace engineers* perform throughout the development, design, and manufacturing processes. The finished product must be evaluated for its reliability, vulnerability, and how it is to be maintained and supported.

Marketing and sales aerospace engineers work with customers, usually industrial corporations and the government, informing them of product performance. They act as a liaison between the technical engineers and the clients to help ensure that the products delivered are performing as planned. Sales engineers also need to anticipate the needs of the customer, as far ahead as possible, to inform their companies of potential marketing opportunities. They also keep abreast of their competitors and need to understand how to structure contracts effectively.

REQUIREMENTS

High School

While in high school, follow a college preparatory program. Doing well in mathematics and science classes is vital if you want to pursue a career in any type of engineering field. The American Society for Engineering Education advises students to take calculus and trigonometry in high school, as well as laboratory science classes. Such courses provide the skills you'll need for problem solving, an essential skill in any type of engineering.

Postsecondary Training

Aerospace engineers need a bachelor's degree to enter the field. More advanced degrees are necessary for those interested in teaching or research and development positions.

While a major in aerospace engineering is the norm, other majors are acceptable. For example, the National Aeronautics and Space Administration recommends a degree in any of a variety of disciplines, including biomedical engineering, ceramics engineering, chemistry, industrial engineering, materials science, metallurgy, optical engineering, and oceanography. You should make sure the college you choose has an accredited engineering program. The Accreditation Board for Engineering and Technology (ABET) sets minimum education standards for programs in these fields. Graduation from an ABET-accredited school is a requirement for becoming licensed in many states, so it is important to select an accredited school. Currently, approximately 1,830 colleges and universities offer ABET-accredited bachelor's of engineering programs. Visit ABET's Web site (http://www.abet.org) for a listing of accredited schools.

Some aerospace engineers complete master's degrees and even doctoral work before entering this field. Advanced degrees can significantly increase an engineer's earnings. Students continuing on to graduate school will study research and development, with a thesis required for a master's degree and a dissertation for a doctorate. About one-third of all aerospace engineers go on to graduate school to get a master's degree.

Certification or Licensing

All states require engineers to be licensed. There are two levels of licensing for engineers. Professional Engineers (PEs) have graduated from an accredited engineering curriculum, have four years of engineering experience, and have passed a written exam. Engineering graduates need not wait until they have four years experience, however, to start the licensure process. Those who pass the Fundamentals of Engineering examination after graduating are called Engineers in Training (EITs) or Engineer Interns or Intern Engineers. The EIT certification usually is valid for 10 years. After acquiring suitable work experience, EITs can take the second examination, the Principles and Practice of Engineering exam, to gain full PE licensure. The exam is administered by the National Council of Examiners for Engineering and Surveying (http://www.ncees.org).

In order to ensure that aerospace engineers are kept up to date on their quickly changing field, many states have imposed continuing education requirements for relicensure.

Other Requirements

Aerospace engineers should enjoy completing detailed work, problem solving, and participating in group efforts. Mathematical, science, and computer skills are a must. Equally important, however, are the abilities to communicate ideas, share in teamwork, and visualize the forms and functions of structures. Curiosity, inventiveness, and the willingness to continue learning from experiences are excellent qualities to have for this type of work.

EXPLORING

If you like to work on model airplanes and rockets, you may be a good candidate for an aerospace engineering career. Consider working on special research assignments supervised by your science and math teachers for helpful experience. You may also want to try working on cars and boats, which provides a good opportunity to discover more about aerodynamics. A part-time job with a local manufacturer can give you some exposure to product engineering and development.

Exciting opportunities are often available at summer camps and academic programs throughout the country. For instance, the University of North Dakota (see address listed at the end of this article) presents an aerospace camp focusing on study and career exploration that includes instruction in model rocketry and flight. However, admission to the camp is competitive; the camp usually consists of two eight-day programs for 32 students each.

It is also a good idea to join a science club while in high school. For example, the Junior Engineering Technical Society provides members with opportunities to enter academic competitions, explore career opportunities, and design model structures. Contact information is available at the end of this article.

Aerospace America (http://www.aerospaceamerica.org/Pages/TableOfContents.aspx), published by the American Institute of Aeronautics and Astronautics, is a helpful magazine for exploring careers in aerospace. You should also check out the American Society for Engineering Education's precollege Web site, http://www.asee.org/k12/, for general information about careers in engineering, as well as answers to frequently asked questions about engineering. In addition, the society offers *Engineering, Go For It!*, a comprehensive brochure about careers for a small fee.

If you are a high school student with an interest in aerospace, you can join the American Institute of Aeronautics and Astronautics. Members receive a magazine, networking opportunities, and discounts on institute products, programs, and services.

EMPLOYERS

The U.S. Department of Labor reports that approximately 71,600 aerospace engineers are employed in the United States. Many aircraft-related engineering jobs are found in Washington, Texas, and Maryland, where large aerospace companies are located. Approximately 49 percent of all aerospace engineers work in products and parts manufacturing. Government agencies such as the Department of Defense and the National Aeronautics and Space Administration also employ a significant number of aerospace engineers. Other employers include engineering services, research and testing services, and electronics manufacturers.

STARTING OUT

Many students begin their careers while completing their studies through work-study arrangements that sometimes turn into full-time jobs. Most aerospace manufacturers actively recruit engineering students, conducting on-campus interviews and other activities to locate the best candidates. Students preparing to graduate can also send out resumes to companies active in the aerospace industry and arrange interviews. Many colleges and universities also staff job placement centers, which are often good places to find leads for new job openings.

Students can also apply directly to agencies of the federal government concerned with aerospace development and implementation. Applications can be made through the Office of Personnel Management or through an agency's own hiring department.

Professional associations, such as the National Society of Professional Engineers and the American Institute of Aeronautics and Astronautics, offer job listings and career resources at their Web sites. Their Web addresses are listed at the end of this article.

ADVANCEMENT

As in most engineering fields, there tends to be a hierarchy of workers in the various divisions of aerospace engineering. This is true in research, design and development, production, and teaching. In an entry-level job, one is considered simply an engineer, perhaps a *junior engineer*. After a certain amount of experience is gained, depending on the position, one moves on to work as a *project engineer*, supervising others. Then, as a *managing engineer*, one has further responsibilities over a number of project engineers and their teams. At the top of the hierarchy is the position of *chief engineer*, which involves authority over managing engineers and additional decision-making responsibilities.

As engineers move up the career ladder, the type of responsibilities they have tend to change. Junior engineers are highly involved in technical matters and scientific problem solving. As managers and chiefs, engineers have the responsibilities of supervising, cost analyzing, and relating with clients.

All engineers must continue to learn and study technological progress throughout their careers. It is important to keep abreast of engineering advancements and trends by reading industry journals and taking courses. Such courses are offered by professional associations or colleges. In aerospace engineering especially, changes occur rapidly, and those who seek promotions must be prepared. Those who are employed by colleges and universities must continue teaching and conducting research if they want to have tenured (more guaranteed) faculty positions.

EARNINGS

In 2008, the median salary for all aerospace engineers was $92,520, according to the U.S. Department of Labor. Experienced engineers employed by the federal government tended to earn more, with a mean salary of $103,810. Federal employees, however, enjoy greater job security and often more generous vacation and retirement benefits. The most experienced aerospace engineers earned salaries of more than $134,570.

Aerospace engineers with bachelor's degrees earned average starting salaries of $53,408 per year in 2007, according to a salary survey conducted by the National Association of Colleges and Employers. With a master's degree, candidates were offered $62,459, and with a Ph.D., $73,814.

All full-time engineers can expect to receive vacation and sick pay, paid holidays, health insurance, life insurance, and retirement programs.

WORK ENVIRONMENT

Aerospace engineers work in various settings depending on their job description. Those involved in research and design usually work in a traditional office setting. They spend considerable time at computers and drawing boards. Engineers involved with the testing of components and structures often work outside at test sites or in laboratories where controlled testing conditions can be created.

In the manufacturing area of the aerospace industry, engineers often work on the factory floor itself, assembling components and making sure that they conform to design specifications. This job requires much walking around large production facilities, such as aircraft factories or spacecraft assembly plants.

Engineers are sometimes required to travel to other locations to consult with companies that make materials and other needed components. Others travel to remote test sites to observe and participate in flight testing.

Aerospace engineers are also employed by the Federal Aviation Administration and commercial airline companies. These engineers perform a variety of duties, including performance analysis and crash investigations. Companies that are involved with satellite communications need the expertise of aerospace engineers to better interpret the many aspects of the space environment and the problems involved with getting a satellite launched into space.

OUTLOOK

Employment in this field is expected to grow about as fast as the average for all occupations through 2018, according to the U.S. Department of Labor.

Growth in the number of military aerospace projects, increasing airline traffic, and the need to replace aging airplanes with quieter and more fuel-efficient aircraft will boost demand for aerospace engineers. The federal government has increased defense budgets in order to build up the armed forces. More aerospace engineers will be needed to repair and add to the current air fleet, as well as to improve defense technology. Engineers are also needed to help make commercial aircraft safer, designing and installing reinforced cockpit doors and onboard security screening equipment to protect pilots, crew, and commercial passengers.

Despite cutbacks in the space program, the development of new space technology and increasing commercial uses for that technology will continue to require qualified engineers. Facing reduced demand in the United States, aerospace companies are increasing their sales overseas, and depending on the world economy and foreign demand, this new market could create a demand for new workers in the industry.

FOR MORE INFORMATION

For a list of accredited schools and colleges, contact
Accreditation Board for Engineering and Technology
111 Market Place, Suite 1050
Baltimore, MD 21202-7116
Tel: 410-347-7700
http://www.abet.org

Contact the AIA for publications with information on aerospace technologies, careers, and space.
Aerospace Industries Association of America (AIA)
1000 Wilson Boulevard, Suite 1700
Arlington, VA 22209-3928
Tel: 703-358-1000
http://www.aia-aerospace.org

For career information and details on membership for high school students, contact
American Institute of Aeronautics and Astronautics
1801 Alexander Bell Drive, Suite 500
Reston, VA 20191-4344
Tel: 800-639-2422
http://www.aiaa.org

For information on educational programs and to purchase a copy of Engineering: Go For It, *contact*
American Society for Engineering Education
1818 N Street, NW, Suite 600
Washington, DC 20036-2479
Tel: 202-331-3500
http://www.asee.org

For information on careers and student competitions, contact
Junior Engineering Technical Society
1420 King Street, Suite 405
Alexandria, VA 22314-2750
Tel: 703-548-5387
E-mail: info@jets.org
http://www.jets.org

For career and licensing information, contact
National Society of Professional Engineers
1420 King Street
Alexandria, VA 22314-2750
Tel: 703-684-2800
http://www.nspe.org/students

SEDS is an international organization of high school and college students dedicated to promoting interest in space. Its U.S. national headquarters are located at the Massachusetts Institute of Technology.
Students for the Exploration and Development of Space (SEDS)
MIT Room W20-445
77 Massachusetts Avenue
Cambridge, MA 02139-4307
E-mail: outreach@seds.org
http://www.seds.org

For information on aerospace programs and summer camps, contact
University of North Dakota
John D. Odegard School of Aerospace Sciences
UND Aerospace
Odegard Hall, Room 200
Grand Forks, ND 58202-9008
Tel: 800-258-1525
E-mail: flyund@aero.und.edu
http://www.aero.und.edu

INTERVIEW

Jennifer Dandrea is a flight test engineer for The Boeing Company. In 2009, she was chosen by the National Engineers Week Foundation as one of the New Faces of Engineering—a group of young engineers from all disciplines who are making special contributions to their respective fields. Jennifer discussed her career with the editors of Careers in Focus: Aviation.

Q. Why did you decide to become an engineer?

A. I decided to be an engineer back in high school. I was always good at math and science and enjoyed auto shop and building things. Engineering was perfect. I studied mechanical engineering at Syracuse University with a minor in energy systems. I wanted to be a design engineer for heating, ventilation, and air-conditioning in energy efficient LEED (Leadership in Energy and Environmental Design) and green buildings, which I did my first job out of college working in New York City. But as opportunities came up, my career path migrated, and I'm now in the aerospace industry.

Q. What are your typical job responsibilities?

A. I work in the Test and Evaluation Organization at Boeing. I'm currently working in Seattle, Washington, on the 787 (Dreamliner) program. My specific job classification is Ground Operations. I'm responsible for preparing testing documents, shop coordination, and test equipment needed for both in-flight and on-the-ground tests. Daily activities include coordinating with the shop for proper layup of the airplane, and ensuring correct conformity (meeting design specification for the Federal Aviation Administration) for testing. Onboard during flight testing, I am the cabin safety focal as well as the weights engineer. For some tests, center of gravity and weight of the airplane is critical, and this needs to be monitored and controlled with either fuel burn changes or ballast moving. As for safety, I'm trained in airplane evacuation, first aid, CPR, and Automatic External Defibulator (this device provides an electrical impulse to restart the heart; they are almost standard in most buildings) if there's an emergency onboard.

Q. What are some of the pros and cons of work as a flight test engineer?

A. I love my job when we fly. There's a lot of soft skills you use when dealing with managers, factory shop, other engineering peers, as well as higher leadership. I really enjoy the people interaction of my job. I'm not just stuck at a desk behind a computer drafting. It is very hands-on where I get to poke around and look at all the systems and equipment in the airplane, as well as test them to ensure they work properly. There is so much to learn. However, I do work in an airplane factory—which isn't as glorious as other jobs. It's loud and noisy. My job is also very mobile. I do a lot of traveling when we are testing, which is fun, but [it is] extremely tiring working almost seven days a week. We have extremely tight schedules to meet and the company depends on it. There's a lot of stress and flexibility involved. Overall, it's a great field and I do enjoy it!

Q. What are the most important personal and professional qualities for engineers?

A. The most important in any job is ethics, especially as an engineer, because many lives are at risk. In flight testing, you are onboard the airplane trying to achieve certification. If you withhold information or know something is not safe, people can be severely hurt. That's a major reason there is the Order of the Engineer (http://www.order-of-the-engineer.org/e-ring.htm), which is similar to the doctor's Hippocratic Oath. The Order is a written obligation of an engineer's responsibilities to the public and to the profession. Having confidence to speak up and the desire for continuous learning will develop one into a great engineer.

Q. What advice would you give to high school students who are interested in this career?

A. If you want to pursue engineering, stock up on math and science classes. It will give you an advantage for college. There are also many programs to get involved with such as Future Cities and First Robotics, along with local boat design competitions (maritime engineers), bridge contests (civil engineers), and rocket and car competitions. The best way to decide if engineering is something you like is to dive into it early.

Q. What are your future career plans?

A. I'm hoping to start heading toward an engineering management path. I just finished my master's in engineering management. I don't see myself staying in flight test due to the nature of the program (it is very cyclical). I want to either go back into building design or possible work for a nonprofit promoting engineering/math/science in schools.

Agricultural Pilots

QUICK FACTS

School Subjects
Mathematics
Physics

Personal Skills
Leadership/management
Technical/scientific

Work Environment
Indoors and outdoors
Primarily multiple locations

Minimum Education Level
Some postsecondary training

Salary Range
$32,020 to $65,340 to
$129,580+

Certification or Licensing
Required by all states

Outlook
Little or no change

DOT
196

GOE
07.03.01

NOC
2271

O*NET-SOC
53-2012.00

OVERVIEW

Agricultural pilots, also called *ag pilots* and *aerial applicators*, perform flying jobs related to the farming industry. They are skilled professionals who operate aircraft for such purposes as transporting cargo to market, aerial applications, hauling feed, or planting seed. In addition to flying aircraft, agricultural pilots are responsible for performing a variety of safety-related tasks involving both the aircraft and the cargo. They may be self-employed or work for large pest control companies or government agencies. There are approximately 3,200 agricultural pilots employed in the United States.

HISTORY

The history of agricultural aviation is, naturally, tied to that of modern aviation. This period is generally considered to have begun with the flight of Orville and Wilbur Wright's heavier-than-air machine on December 17, 1903. On that day, the Wright brothers flew their machine four times and became the first airplane pilots. In the early days of aviation, the pilot's job was quite different from that of the pilot of today. As he flew the plane, for example, Orville Wright was lying on his stomach in the middle of the bottom wing of the plane. There was a strap across his hips, and to turn the plane, he had to tilt his hips from side to side—hardly the way today's pilot makes a turn.

The aviation industry developed rapidly as designers raced to improve upon the Wright brothers' design. During the early years of flight, many aviators earned a living as "barnstormers," entertaining people with stunts and taking passengers on short flights around the countryside. As airplanes became more dependable, they were adapted for a variety of purposes such as use in the military and for the U.S. government-run airmail service. According to the National Agricultural Aviation Association, the first time a plane was used to spread pesticide was in 1921. In an experiment conducted by the military, lead arsenate dust was spread by plane to stop a moth infestation in Ohio. By 1923 crop dusting was being done on a commercial basis.

Today planes used for agricultural aviation are specifically designed for that purpose. They can carry hundreds of gallons of pesticides and are equipped with the latest technology, such as the Global Positioning System (GPS). Unlike the crop-dusting process of the past, which used dry chemicals, today's process typically involves liquid pesticides and other controlling products as well as nutrition sprays. Advances in agricultural aviation have allowed U.S. farms to become increasingly productive.

THE JOB

Agricultural pilots perform a number of duties that benefit the farming industry. They assist farmers in the prevention of crop damage. Some work for pest control companies while others are self-employed. In farm work, agricultural pilots spray chemicals over crops and orchards to fertilize them, control plant diseases or weeds, and control pests. They also drop seeds into fields to plant crops.

Before agricultural pilots begin the process of spraying farmland, they must survey the area for buildings, hills, power lines, and other obstacles and hazards. They must also notify residents and businesses in the general area that they will spray so that people and animals can be moved away from target areas.

Some agricultural pilots, particularly those who work for pest control companies, may mix their own chemicals, using their knowledge of what mixture may be best for certain types of plants, plant or soil conditions, or pest problems.

Agricultural pilots fly helicopters and small, turboprop planes, which are slower compared to larger, transport craft, but which are good for flying close to the ground and for carrying heavy loads. They must fly close to the ground, often only a few feet above a crop, so that they will only hit designated areas with the chemicals.

Agricultural pilots help farmers by dropping food over pastures. They may photograph wildlife or count game animals for conservation programs. And their work also extends into forests, fields, and swamps, where herbicides and insecticides are needed. They also fight forest fires by dumping water or fire-retardant materials over burning areas.

No matter what the job, pilots must determine weather and flight conditions, make sure that sufficient fuel is on board to complete the flight safely, and verify the maintenance status of the airplane before each flight. They perform system checks to test the proper functioning of instrumentation and electronic and mechanical systems on the plane.

Once all of these preflight duties are done, the pilot taxis the aircraft to the designated runway and prepares for takeoff. Takeoff speeds must be calculated based on the aircraft's weight, which is affected by the weight of the cargo being carried.

During flights, agricultural pilots must constantly be aware of their surroundings since they fly so close to the ground and frequently are near hazards such as power lines. They need good judgment to deal with any emergency situations that might arise. They monitor aircraft systems, keep an eye on the weather conditions, and perform the job of the flight, such as spraying fertilizer.

Once the pilot has landed and taxied to the appropriate area, he or she follows a "shutdown" checklist of procedures. Pilots also keep logs of their flight hours. Those who are self-employed or work for smaller companies are typically responsible for refueling the airplane, performing maintenance, and keeping business records.

Did You Know?

- Ninety percent of agricultural pilots own their own businesses.
- The average agricultural pilot has more than 20 years of experience in the field.
- Agricultural pilots fly helicopters and fixed-wing aircraft that cost anywhere from $100,000 to $1.4 million. These aircraft are well built in order to handle 30 to 100 takeoffs and landings each day.
- Agricultural pilots are sometimes called crop dusters, but this is not an accurate name for today's pilots. Many aerial applications today are now in liquid form, and agricultural pilots also plant seeds, apply fertilizer, and fight fires in addition to applying pesticides to farmland.

Source: National Agricultural Aviation Association

REQUIREMENTS

High School

There are a number of classes you can take in high school to help prepare you for becoming a pilot. You should take science classes, such as chemistry and physics, as well as mathematics, such as algebra and geometry. Take computer classes to familiarize yourself with various programs. Since you will be responsible for the maintenance and care of a plane, you may also benefit from taking an electronics shop class or other shop class where you get to work on engines. Take English classes to improve your research and writing skills. Throughout your career you will need to study flying or repair manuals, file reports, and communicate with customers. Since you may be responsible for record keeping, take business or accounting classes. If your school offers agriculture classes, take any that will teach you about soils, crops, and growing methods.

Postsecondary Training

Many companies that employ pilots prefer to hire candidates with at least two years of college training. Courses in engineering, meteorology, physics, mathematics, and agriculture are helpful in preparing for this career. In addition to these courses, you will need training as a pilot. There are approximately 600 civilian flying schools certified by the Federal Aviation Administration (FAA), including some colleges and universities that offer degree credit for pilot training. A number of schools offer training specifically in agricultural aviation. Some people take up this career after leaving the military, where they trained as pilots.

The National Agricultural Aviation Association offers information on training requirements and schools at its Web site, http://www.agaviation.org.

Certification or Licensing

Agricultural pilots must hold a commercial pilot's license from the FAA. A fairly long and rigorous process is involved in obtaining a commercial license. The first step in this process is to receive flying instruction.

If you are 16 or over and can pass the rigid mandatory physical examination, you may apply for permission to take flying instruction. This instruction consists of classroom education and flight training from a FAA-certified flight instructor.

Before you make your first solo flight, you must get a medical certificate (certifying that you are in good health) and an instructor-endorsed student pilot certificate. In order to get the student pilot certificate, you must pass a test given by the flight instructor. This test will have questions about FAA rules as well as questions about the model and make of the aircraft you will fly. If you pass the test and the instructor feels you are prepared to make a solo flight, the instructor will endorse your pilot certificate and logbook.

To apply for a private pilot's license, you must take a written examination. To qualify for it, you must be at least 17 years of age, successfully fulfill a solo flying requirement of 20 hours or more, and meet instrument flying and cross-country flying requirements.

The next step in getting a commercial license is to continue to log flying time and increase your knowledge and skills. To receive your commercial license you must be at least 18 years of age, have 250 hours of flying time, and successfully complete a number of exams. These tests include a physical exam; a written test given by the FAA covering such topics as safe flight operations, navigation principles, and federal aviation regulations; and a practical test to demonstrate your flying skills. Pilots must also receive a rating for the kind of plane they can fly (such as single-engine or multiengine). In addition, a commercial pilot needs an instrument rating by the FAA and a restricted radiotelephone operator's permit by the Federal Communications Commission (FCC). In states where restricted pesticides are sprayed, agricultural pilots must be certified by the U.S. Department of Agriculture.

Other Requirements

All pilots must be of sound physical and emotional health. They need excellent eyesight and eye-hand coordination as well as excellent hearing and normal heart rate and blood pressure. The successful agricultural pilot is also detail-oriented since much paperwork, planning, and following of regulations is involved in this job. Those who are self-employed or working for smaller companies may find that they have frequent contact with customers, and so they must be able to work well with others. Naturally, an agricultural pilot should have an interest in farming methods and the environment as well as a love of flying. Good judgment is essential for this work.

EXPLORING

You can explore this field through a number of activities. Join groups such as your high school aviation club and the National FFA Organization (formerly Future Farmers of America). These groups may give you the opportunity to meet with professionals in the field, learn about farm products and management, and find others with similar interests. Read publications related to these industries such as the magazines *Agricultural Aviation* (http://www.agaviation.org/agmag.htm), *AgAir Update* (http://www.agairupdate.com), and *The Progressive Farmer* (http://progressivefarmer.com). If you have the financial resources, you can take flying lessons once you are 16 and have passed a physical exam. Also, consider learning how to operate a ham radio. This skill will help you when you apply for your restricted radio operator's permit, a requirement for commercial pilots.

EMPLOYERS

Approximately 3,200 agricultural pilots are employed in the United States. California and the southern states, where the crop-growing season lasts longest, are where agricultural pilots find the most work. They also find some work with northern crops and in forests of the northeastern and western states. Many are employed by crop-dusting companies, while others are self-employed. Federal and state government departments also employ agricultural pilots to assist with environmental, conservation, and preservation needs.

STARTING OUT

It is not unusual for people to enter this field after gaining experience in the agricultural industry itself, working on farms and learning about crop production while they also develop their flying skills. Others enter with flying as their first love and are drawn to the challenge of agricultural aviation. Once pilots have completed their training, they may find that contacts made through aviation schools lead to job openings. Those who have the financial means can begin by opening their own business. Equipment, however, is very expensive—a single plane appropriately outfitted can cost anywhere from $100,000 to $1.4 million. A number of people, therefore, begin by working for large aerial applications companies before they strike out on their own.

The National Agricultural Aviation Association offers job listings at its Web site, http://www.agaviation.org/careers.htm.

ADVANCEMENT

Agricultural pilots who work for a company can be promoted to manager. Self-employed agricultural pilots move up by charging more money for their services and increasing their client base. Another way to advance is to work in other areas of commercial aviation. These pilots may fly cargo and people to remote locations or become aerial photographers.

EARNINGS

Median salaries for full-time commercial pilots (a category that includes agricultural pilots) were $65,340 in 2008, according to the U.S. Department of Labor. Salaries ranged from less than $32,020 to $129,580 or more. Agricultural pilots who are employed by companies rarely get paid for vacation days and only a few companies offer health and accident insurance and profit-sharing and pension plans.

WORK ENVIRONMENT

The vast majority of an agricultural pilot's job takes place outdoors, during the early morning and early evening hours. Their work is demanding and can be hazardous. When flying, agricultural pilots wear safety gear consisting of a helmet, safety belt, and shoulder harness, because they fly under such difficult conditions. They fly close to the ground in populated areas and must be cautious to avoid obstacles. They also face exposure to pesticides and other harsh substances. When mixing or loading chemicals onto the plane, they sometimes wear gloves or masks to prevent the inhaling of harmful vapors.

OUTLOOK

Employment opportunities for experienced agricultural pilots are expected to remain about the same for the next decade. However, the demand for agricultural pilots depends largely on farmers' needs. For example, during times when insect and pest control becomes a problem, there is greater demand for agricultural pilots. There is also some concern within the industry that genetically engineered crops (resistant to certain diseases) may decrease the need for aerial applications and cause a loss of business for agricultural pilots. Keeping these factors in mind, employment prospects will probably be best with larger farms and ranches and in states with long growing seasons.

FOR MORE INFORMATION

This organization has information on crop protection products and developments in the industry.

CropLife America
1156 15th Street, NW
Washington, DC 20005-1704
Tel: 202-296-1585
http://www.croplifeamerica.org

Visit the association's Web site to read Ag Aviation Careers: How
to Become an Ag Pilot.
National Agricultural Aviation Association
1005 E Street, SE
Washington, DC 20003-2847
Tel: 202-546-5722
E-mail: information@agaviation.org
http://www.agaviation.org

*For information on opportunities in the agricultural field and local
chapters, contact*
National FFA Organization
National FFA Center
6060 FFA Drive
PO Box 68960
Indianapolis, IN 46268-0960
Tel: 317-802-6060
http://www.ffa.org

Aircraft Mechanics

QUICK FACTS

School Subjects
Computer science
Technical/shop

Personal Skills
Mechanical/manipulative
Technical/scientific

Work Environment
Indoors and outdoors
One location with some travel

Minimum Education Level
Some postsecondary
training

Salary Range
$32,960 to $51,390 to
$69,030+

Certification or Licensing
Recommended

Outlook
Decline

DOT
621

GOE
05.03.01

NOC
2244, 7315

O*NET-SOC
49-2091.00, 49-3011.00,
49-3011.01, 49-3011.02,
49-3011.03

OVERVIEW

Aircraft mechanics examine, service, repair, and overhaul aircraft and aircraft engines. They also repair, replace, and assemble parts of the airframe (the structural parts of the plane other than the power plant or engine). There are about 121,500 aircraft mechanics working in the United States.

HISTORY

On December 17, 1903, Wilbur and Orville Wright made history's first successful powered flight. The Wright brothers—who originally built and repaired bicycles—designed, built, and repaired their airplane, including the engine, making them the first airplane mechanics as well. In the early years of aviation, most airplane designers filled a similar scope of functions, although many had people to assist them. As the aviation industry grew, the various tasks required to design, build, operate, and repair aircraft became more specialized. However, because of the instability of early planes and the uncertainty of the weather and other conditions, it was often necessary for pilots to have a strong working knowledge of how to repair and maintain their aircraft. In later years, one important route to becoming a pilot was to start as an aircraft mechanic.

As aircraft became capable of flying faster, for longer distances, and at higher altitudes, and especially after aircraft began to carry passengers, the role of the aircraft mechanic became vital to the safety of the aircraft and the growth of the aviation industry. New technologies have continually been introduced into the design of aircraft, and mechanics needed to be familiar with all the systems, from the airframe to the engine to the control systems. The complexity of airplane design increased to the point where the mechanics themselves began to specialize. Some mechanics had the skills to work on the entire aircraft. Others were able to work on the airframe, on the engines, or on the power plant. Some mechanics functioned as repairers, who completed minor repairs to the plane. Mechanics were assisted by technicians, who were often training to become fully qualified mechanics. With the introduction of electronics into aircraft, some mechanics specialized as avionics technicians.

The Air Commerce Act of 1926 imposed regulations on the commercial airlines and their fleets. The Federal Aviation Agency, later called the Federal Aviation Administration (FAA), also established training and licensing requirements for the mechanics servicing the airplanes. Mechanics were also an important part of the armed forces, especially during World War II, in which air power became a vital part of successful military operations.

The growth of the general aviation industry, which includes all flights operated outside of the airlines, provided still more demand for trained mechanics. The introduction of ultralight aircraft in the 1970s brought air flight back to its origins: these craft were often sold as kits that the purchasers had to build and repair themselves.

THE JOB

The work of aircraft mechanics employed by the commercial airlines may be classified into two categories, that of *line maintenance mechanics* and *overhaul mechanics*.

Line maintenance mechanics are all-around craft workers who make repairs on all parts of the plane. Working at the airport, they make emergency and other necessary repairs in the time between when aircraft land and when they take off again. They may be told by the pilot, flight engineer, or head mechanic what repairs need to be made, or they may thoroughly inspect the plane themselves for oil leaks, cuts or dents in the surface and tires, or any malfunction in the radio, radar, and light equipment. In addition, their duties include changing oil, cleaning spark plugs, and replenishing the hydraulic and oxygen systems. They work as fast as safety permits so the aircraft can be put back into service quickly.

Overhaul mechanics keep the aircraft in top operating condition by performing scheduled maintenance, making repairs, and conducting inspections required by the FAA. Scheduled maintenance programs are based on the number of hours flown, calendar days, or a combination of these factors. Overhaul mechanics work at the airline's main overhaul base on either or both of the two major parts of the aircraft: the airframe, which includes wings, fuselage, tail assembly, landing gear, control cables, propeller assembly, and fuel and oil tanks; or the power plant, which may be a radial (internal combustion), turbojet, turboprop, or rocket engine.

Airframe mechanics work on parts of the aircraft other than the engine, inspecting the various components of the airframe for worn or defective parts. They check the sheet-metal surfaces, measure the tension of control cables, and check for rust, distortion, and cracks in the fuselage and wings. They consult manufacturers' manuals and the airline's maintenance manual for specifications and to determine whether repair or replacement is needed to correct defects or malfunctions. They also use specialized computer software to assist them in determining the need, extent, and nature of repairs. Airframe mechanics repair, replace, and assemble parts using a variety of tools, including power shears, sheet-metal breakers, arc and acetylene welding equipment, rivet guns, and air or electric drills.

Aircraft power plant mechanics inspect, service, repair, and overhaul the engine of the aircraft. Looking through specially designed openings while working from ladders or scaffolds, they examine an engine's external appearance for such problems as cracked cylinders, oil leaks, or cracks or breaks in the turbine blades. They also listen to the engine in operation to detect sounds indicating malfunctioning components, such as sticking or burned valves. The test equipment used to check the engine's operation includes ignition analyzers, compression checkers, distributor timers, and ammeters. If necessary, the mechanics remove the engine from the aircraft, using a hoist or a forklift truck, and take the engine apart. They use sensitive instruments to measure parts for wear and use X-ray and magnetic inspection equipment to check for invisible cracks. Worn or damaged parts are replaced or repaired, then the mechanics reassemble and reinstall the engine.

Aircraft mechanics adjust and repair electrical wiring systems and aircraft accessories and instruments; inspect, service, and repair pneumatic and hydraulic systems; and handle various servicing tasks, such as flushing crankcases, cleaning screens, greasing moving parts, and checking brakes.

Mechanics may work on only one type of aircraft or on many different types, such as jets, propeller-driven planes, and helicopters. For greater efficiency, some specialize in one section, such as the electrical system, of a particular type of aircraft. Among the specialists, there are airplane electricians; pneumatic testers and pressure sealer-and-testers; aircraft body repairers and bonded structures repairers, such as burnishers and bumpers; and air-conditioning mechanics, aircraft rigging and controls mechanics, plumbing and hydraulics mechanics, and experimental-aircraft testing mechanics. *Avionics technicians* are mechanics who specialize in the aircraft's electronic systems.

Mechanics who work for businesses that own their own aircraft usually handle all necessary repair and maintenance work. The planes, however, generally are small and the work is less complex than in repair shops.

In small, independent repair shops, mechanics must inspect and repair many different types of aircraft. The airplanes may include small commuter planes run by an aviation company, private company planes and jets, private individually owned aircraft, and planes used for flying instruction.

REQUIREMENTS

High School
The first requirement for prospective aircraft mechanics is a high school diploma. Courses in mathematics, physics, chemistry, and mechanical drawing are particularly helpful because they teach the principles involved in the operation of an aircraft, and this knowledge is often necessary to making the repairs. Machine shop, auto mechanics, or electrical shop are important courses for gaining many skills needed by aircraft mechanics.

Postsecondary Training
At one time, mechanics were able to acquire their skills through on-the-job training. This is rare today. Now most mechanics learn the job either in the armed forces or in trade schools approved by the FAA. The trade schools provide training with the necessary tools and equipment in programs that range in length from 18 to 24 months. In considering applicants for certification, the FAA sometimes accepts successful completion of such schooling in place of work experience, but the schools do not guarantee an FAA certificate. There are about 170 such schools in the United States.

The experience acquired by aircraft mechanics in the armed forces sometimes satisfies the work requirements for FAA certification, and veterans may be able to pass the exam with a limited amount of additional study. But jobs in the military service are usually too specialized to satisfy the FAA requirement for broad work experience. In that case, veterans applying for FAA approval will have to complete a training program at a trade school. Schools occasionally give some credit for material learned in the service. However, on the plus side, airlines are especially eager to hire aircraft mechanics with both military experience and a trade school education.

Certification or Licensing

FAA certification is necessary for certain types of aircraft mechanics and is usually required to advance beyond entry-level positions. Most mechanics who work on civilian aircraft have FAA authorization as airframe mechanics, power plant mechanics, or avionics repair specialists. Airframe mechanics are qualified to work on the fuselage, wings, landing gear, and other structural parts of the aircraft; power plant mechanics are qualified for work on the engine. Mechanics may qualify for both airframe and power plant licensing, allowing them to work on any part of the plane. Combination airframe and power plant mechanics with an inspector's certificate are permitted to certify inspection work done by other mechanics. Mechanics without certification must be supervised by certified mechanics.

FAA certification is granted only to aircraft mechanics with previous work experience: a minimum of 18 months for an airframe or power plant certificate and at least 30 months working with both engines and airframes for a combination certificate. To qualify for an inspector's certificate, mechanics must have held a combined airframe and power plant certificate for at least three years. In addition, all applicants for certification must pass written and oral tests and demonstrate their ability to do the work authorized by the certificate.

Other Requirements

Aircraft mechanics must be able to work with precision and meet rigid standards. Their physical condition is also important. They need more than average strength for lifting heavy parts and tools, as well as agility for reaching and climbing. And they should not be afraid of heights, since they may work on top of the wings and fuselages of large jet planes.

In addition to education and certification, union membership may be a requirement for some jobs, particularly for mechanics employed by major airlines. The principal unions organizing aircraft mechanics are the International Association of Machinists and Aerospace Workers and the Transport Workers Union of America. In addition, some mechanics are represented by the International Brotherhood of Teamsters.

EXPLORING

Working with electronic kits, tinkering with automobile engines, and assembling model airplanes are good ways of gauging your ability to do the kinds of work performed by aircraft mechanics. A guided tour of an airfield can give you a brief overall view of this industry. Even better would be a part-time or summer job with an airline in an area such as the baggage department. Small airports may also offer job opportunities for part-time, summer, or replacement workers. You may also earn a Student Pilot certificate at the age of 16 and may gain more insight into the basic workings of an airplane that way. Kits for building ultralight craft are also available and may provide even more insight into the importance of proper maintenance and repair.

EMPLOYERS

Of the roughly 121,500 aircraft mechanics currently employed in the United States, more than half work for air transportation companies, according to the U.S. Department of Labor. Each airline usually has one main overhaul base, where most of its mechanics are employed. These bases are found along the main airline routes or near large cities, including New York, Chicago, Los Angeles, Atlanta, San Francisco, and Miami.

About 16 percent of aircraft mechanics work for the federal government. Many of these mechanics are civilians employed at military aviation installations, while others work for the FAA, mainly in Oklahoma City, Atlantic City, Wichita, and Washington, D.C. About 14 percent of mechanics work for aircraft assembly firms. Most of the rest are general aviation mechanics employed by independent repair shops at airports around the country, by businesses that use their own planes for transporting employees or cargo, by certified supplemental airlines, or by crop-dusting and air-taxi firms.

STARTING OUT

High school graduates who wish to become aircraft mechanics may enter this field by enrolling in an FAA-approved trade school. (Note that there are schools offering this training that do not have FAA approval.) These schools generally have placement services available for their graduates.

Another method is to make direct application to the employment offices of companies providing air transportation and services or the local offices of the state employment service, although airlines prefer to employ people who have already completed training. Many airports are managed by private fixed-base operators, which also operate the airport's repair and maintenance facilities. The field may also be entered through enlistment in the armed forces.

ADVANCEMENT

Promotions depend in part on the size of the organization for which an aircraft mechanic works. The first promotion after beginning employment is usually based on merit and comes in the form of a salary increase. To advance further, many companies require the mechanic to have a combined airframe and power plant certificate, or perhaps an aircraft inspector's certificate.

Advancement could take the following route: journeyworker mechanic, head mechanic or crew chief, inspector, head inspector, and shop supervisor. With additional training, a mechanic may advance to engineering, administrative, or executive positions. In larger airlines, mechanics may advance to become flight engineers, then copilots and pilots. With business training, some mechanics open their own repair shops.

EARNINGS

Although some aircraft mechanics, especially at the entry level and at small businesses, earn little more than the minimum wage, the median annual income for aircraft mechanics was about $51,390 in 2008, according to the U.S. Department of Labor. The top paid 10 percent earned more than $69,030, while the bottom paid 10 percent earned $32,960 or less. Mechanics with airframe and power plant certification earn more than those without it. Overtime, night shift, and holiday pay differentials are usually available and can greatly increase a mechanic's annual earnings.

Most major airlines are covered by union agreements. Their mechanics generally earn more than those working for other employers. Contracts usually include health insurance and often life insurance and retirement plans as well. An attractive fringe benefit for airline mechanics and their immediate families is free or reduced fares on their own and many other airlines. Mechanics working for the federal government also benefit from the greater job security of civil service and government jobs.

WORK ENVIRONMENT

Most aircraft mechanics work a five-day, 40-hour week. Their working hours, however, may be irregular and often include nights, weekends, and holidays, as airlines operate 24 hours a day, and extra work is required during holiday seasons.

When doing overhauling and major inspection work, aircraft mechanics generally work in hangars with adequate heat, ventilation, and lights. If the hangars are full, however, or if repairs must be made quickly, they may work outdoors, sometimes in unpleasant weather. Outdoor work is frequent for line maintenance mechanics, who work at airports, because they must make minor repairs and preflight checks at the terminal to save time. To maintain flight schedules, or to keep from inconveniencing customers in general aviation, the mechanics often have to work under time pressure.

The work is physically strenuous and demanding. Mechanics often have to lift or pull as much as 70 pounds of weight. They may stand, lie, or kneel in awkward positions, sometimes in precarious places such as on a scaffold or ladder.

Noise and vibration are common when testing engines. Regardless of the stresses and strains, aircraft mechanics are expected to work quickly and with great precision.

Although the power tools and test equipment are provided by the employer, mechanics may be expected to furnish their own hand tools.

OUTLOOK

Employment of aircraft mechanics is likely to decline through 2018, according to the U.S. Department of Labor. The demand for air travel and the numbers of aircraft created are expected to increase due to population growth and rising incomes. However, employment growth will be affected by the use of automated systems that make the aircraft mechanic's job more efficient.

Despite recent fluctuations in air travel, the outlook for aircraft mechanics should remain steady over the course of the next decade. Employment opportunities will open up due to fewer young workers entering the labor force, fewer entrants from the military, and more retirees leaving positions. But the job prospects will vary according to the type of employer. Less competition for jobs is likely to be found at smaller commuter and regional airlines, FAA repair stations, and in general aviation. These employers pay lower wages and fewer applicants compete for their positions, while higher paying airline positions, which also include travel benefits, are more in demand among qualified applicants. Mechanics who keep up with technological advancements in electronics, composite materials, and other areas will be in greatest demand.

Opportunities should not be as strong with the federal government. The government is increasingly outsourcing repair work to private contractors, which will reduce employment demand.

FOR MORE INFORMATION

For information on training, careers, and certification, contact
Federal Aviation Administration
800 Independence Avenue, SW
Washington, DC 20591-0001
Tel: 866-835-5322
http://jobs.faa.gov

For information on aviation maintenance and scholarships for college students, contact
Professional Aviation Maintenance Association
400 North Washington Street, Suite 300
Alexandria, VA 22314-2367
Tel: 703-778-4647
E-mail: hq@pama.org
http://www.pama.org

Airline Dispatchers

OVERVIEW

Airplane dispatchers plan and direct commercial air flights according to government and airline company regulations. They read radio reports from airplane pilots during flights and study weather reports to determine any necessary change in flight direction or altitude. They send instructions by radio to the pilots in the case of heavy storms, fog, mechanical difficulties, or other emergencies. Airline dispatchers are sometimes called *flight superintendents*. The Airline Dispatchers Federation has approximately 1,100 members.

HISTORY

Commercial air service took off slowly in the United States. The first airmail flight occurred in 1911. The first passenger air service was organized in 1914, providing air transportation from Tampa to St. Petersburg, Florida, but this service lasted only six months. In 1917, however, the U.S. Post Office began its first airmail service. In 1925, the Kelly Air Mail Act turned over the airmail routes to 12 private contractors. This formed the basis of the commercial airline industry in the United States.

The airline industry developed rapidly in the years leading up to World War II. The Air Commerce Act of 1926 introduced licensing requirements for pilots and airlines and created a network of defined airways. Improvements in airplane design had brought larger, more comfortable airplanes, and the numbers of passengers reached into the millions. By 1933, the United States boasted the busiest airports in the world.

These developments created a need for people to organize and guide the increasing numbers of flights operated by the airlines. During the early days of aviation, the airplane dispatcher served in a number of capacities, including that of station manager, meteorologist, radio operator, and even mechanic. Often pilots were pressed into service as dispatchers because of their knowledge of weather and of the needs of flight crews. As the airline industry grew, these tasks became specialized. The first federal air traffic control center was opened in 1936. In 1938, federal licensing requirements were established for the airline's own dispatchers. Soon dispatchers were located all over the country.

Since that time, the work of dispatchers has become more involved and complicated, and the airline industry has relied on them extensively to make a major contribution to the safety of commercial air travel. Advancements in technology have eased parts of the airplane dispatcher's job and have also allowed the airlines to consolidate their remote dispatch offices to a smaller number of centrally located offices.

THE JOB

Airplane dispatchers are employed by commercial airlines, and they maintain a constant watch on factors affecting the movement of planes during flights. Dispatchers are responsible for the safety of flights and for making certain that they are operated on an efficient, profit-making basis. The work of dispatchers, however, is not the same as that of air traffic controllers, who are employees of the federal government.

Airplane dispatchers are responsible for giving the company's clearance for each flight that takes off during their shift. Their judgments are based on data received from a number of different sources. In their efforts to make certain that each flight will end successfully, they must take into consideration current weather conditions, weather forecasts, wind speed and direction, and other information. Before flights, they must decide whether the airplane crew should report to the field or whether the airline should begin notifying passengers that their flight has been delayed or canceled. Dispatchers may also have to determine whether an alternate route should be used, either to include another stop for passengers or to avoid certain weather conditions.

Upon reporting to the field before a flight, the pilot confers with the dispatcher and determines the best route to use, the amount of fuel to be placed aboard the aircraft, the altitude at which to fly, and the approximate flying time. The pilot and the dispatcher must agree on the conditions of the flight, and both have the option of delaying or canceling flights should conditions become too hazardous to ensure a safe trip.

Dispatchers may also be responsible for maintaining records and for determining the weight and balance of the aircraft after loading. They must be certain that all intended cargo is loaded aboard each of the appropriate flights. They must also be certain that all their decisions, such as those about the cargo, are in keeping with the safety regulations of the Federal Aviation Administration (FAA), as well as with the rules established by their own airline.

Once the planes are in the air, dispatchers keep in constant contact with the flight crews. A dispatcher may be responsible for communications with as many as 10 or 12 flights at any one time. Contact is maintained through a company-owned radio network that enables each company to keep track of all of its planes. Dispatchers keep the crews informed about the weather that they will encounter, and they record the positions and other information reported by the planes while they are en route. If an emergency occurs, dispatchers coordinate the actions taken in response to the emergency.

Following each flight, the pilot checks with the dispatcher for a debriefing. In the debriefing, the pilot brings the dispatcher up to date about the weather encountered in the air and other conditions related to the flight, so that the dispatcher will have this information available in scheduling subsequent flights.

Good judgment is an important tool of airplane dispatchers, for they must be able to make fast, workable, realistic decisions. Because of this, dispatchers often experience strains and tensions on the job, especially when many flights are in the air or when an emergency occurs.

In larger airlines, there is a certain degree of specialization among dispatchers. An assistant dispatcher may work with the chief dispatcher and have the major responsibility for just one phase of the dispatching activities, such as analyzing current weather information, while a senior dispatcher may be designated to take care of another phase, such as monitoring the operating costs of each flight.

REQUIREMENTS

High School

Some college education is required to be an airplane dispatcher, so if you are interested in this career you should follow a college prep curriculum. Business administration and computer skills are vital to the job, so take any courses available in those subjects. While in high school, you can also pursue a student pilot's license, which is a great advantage, though not a requirement.

Postsecondary Training

Airplane dispatchers are required to have at least two years of college education with studies in meteorology or air transportation. Two years of work experience in air transportation may take the place of the college requirement. Airlines prefer college graduates who have studied mathematics, physics, or meteorology.

There are a few schools around the country that offer dispatcher training. For information on these courses, contact the Airline Dispatchers Federation or visit its Web site at http://www.dispatcher.org.

Certification or Licensing

Airplane dispatchers must be licensed by the FAA. You may prepare for the FAA licensing examination in several different ways. You may work at least one year in a dispatching office under a licensed dispatcher, complete an FAA-approved airline dispatcher's course at a specialized school or training center, or show that you have spent two of the previous three years in air traffic control work or a related job.

Candidates who meet the preliminary requirements must also pass an examination covering such subjects as civil air regulations, radio procedures, airport and airway traffic procedures, weather analysis, and air-navigation facilities. In addition to a written test, you must also pass an oral examination covering the interpretation of weather information, landing and cruising speeds of various aircraft, airline routes, navigation facilities, and operational characteristics of different types of aircraft. You must not only demonstrate your knowledge of these areas to become a licensed dispatcher, but you are also expected to maintain these skills once licensed. Various training programs, some of which may be conducted by employers, will assist you in staying current with new developments, which are frequent in this job.

Assistant dispatchers are not always required to be licensed. Thus, it may be possible to begin work in a dispatcher's office prior to earning the dispatcher's license.

Other Requirements

Airline dispatchers need to be able to work well either by themselves or with others and assume responsibility for their decisions. The job requires you to think and act quickly and sensibly under the most trying conditions. You may be responsible for hundreds of lives at any one time, and a poor decision could result in tragedy.

Airline dispatchers must meet minimum age requirements and be in good health. Your vision must be correctable to 20/20. A good memory, the ability to remain calm under great pressure and the ability to do many things at once, and to make decisions quickly are essential to a successful airplane dispatcher's career.

EXPLORING

Besides pursuing the course of study mentioned previously, there is little opportunity for an individual to explore the field of airplane dispatching directly. Part-time or summer jobs with airlines may provide interested students with a chance to observe some of the activities related to dispatching work. You can cultivate your interest in aircraft and aviation through reading and participating in flying clubs.

EMPLOYERS

The Airline Dispatchers Federation has approximately 1,100 members. The larger airlines employ the majority of dispatchers. Smaller airlines and some private firms also employ airplane dispatchers, but the number of dispatchers remains very small. Virtually all airplane dispatchers are employed by commercial airlines, both those that ship cargo and those that transport passengers.

STARTING OUT

The occupation is not easy to enter because of its relatively small size and the special skills required. The nature of the training is such that it is not easily put to use outside of this specific area. Few people leave this career once they are in it, so only a few positions other than those caused by death or retirement become available.

People who are able to break into the field are often promoted to assistant dispatchers' jobs from related fields. They may come from among the airline's dispatch clerks, meteorologists, radio operators, or retired pilots. Obviously, airlines prefer those people who have had a long experience in ground-flight operations work. Thus, it is probably wise to plan on starting out in one of these related fields and eventually working into a position as an airplane dispatcher.

According to the Airline Dispatchers Federation, new graduates from dispatch schools should not expect to be hired by major airlines such as American or United. A better choice would be to seek a position with a smaller carrier and get at least five years' experience before attempting to apply for a position with a major airline.

ADVANCEMENT

The usual path of advancement is from dispatch clerk to assistant dispatcher to dispatcher and then, possibly, to chief flight dispatcher or flight dispatch manager or assistant manager. It is also possible to become a chief flight supervisor or superintendent of flight control.

The line of advancement varies depending on the airline, the size of the facility where the dispatcher is located, and the positions available. At smaller facilities, there may be only two or three different promotional levels available.

EARNINGS

Mean annual earnings for dispatchers employed in scheduled air transportation were $55,270 in 2008, according to the U.S. Department of Labor. Salaries for all dispatchers ranged from less than $20,930 to more than $56,750. Dispatcher salaries vary greatly among airlines. Senior dispatchers at major airlines earn more than $100,000 a year. A few dispatchers earn close to $150,000 including overtime pay.

Airline positions generally provide health insurance and other benefits. Beginning dispatchers usually work eight-hour shifts five days a week and receive two weeks of paid vacation per year. Senior dispatchers usually work four 10-hour shifts a week and may receive as many as six weeks of vacation each year. Most dispatchers and their families are also able to fly for free or at heavily discounted prices.

WORK ENVIRONMENT

Airplane dispatchers are normally stationed at airports near a terminal or hangar, but in facilities away from the public. Some airlines use several dispatch installations, while others use a single office. Because dispatchers make decisions involving not only thousands of people but also a great deal of money, their offices are often located close to those of management, so that they can remain in close contact.

Frequently, the offices where airplane dispatchers work are full of noise and activity, with telephones ringing and many people talking and moving about to consult charts and other sources of information. The offices usually operate 24 hours per day, with each dispatcher working eight-hour shifts, plus an additional half-hour used in briefing the relief person.

Many lives depend on airplane dispatchers every day. This means that there is often considerable stress in their jobs. Dispatchers must constantly make rapid decisions based on their evaluation of a great deal of information. Adding to the tension is the fact that they may work in noisy, hectic surroundings and must interact with many people throughout the day. However, dispatchers can feel deep satisfaction in knowing that their job is vital to the safety and success of airline operations.

OUTLOOK

The Airline Dispatchers Federation says the job market for dispatchers is currently fair, with opportunities being better at smaller commuter airlines. The centralization of dispatch offices using more advanced technology means that fewer dispatchers will be able to do more work. With improved communications equipment, a single dispatcher will be able to cover a larger area than is currently possible. Because of the relatively small size of this occupational field, its employment outlook is not particularly good.

Most major airlines consider dispatch positions as senior management positions. Candidates are often selected from within the company after they have accumulated 15 to 20 years of experience in a variety of areas, including supervisory positions. Candidates selected from outside the company must have considerable experience with smaller carriers.

FOR MORE INFORMATION

For career information, contact
  Airline Dispatchers Federation
  2020 Pennsylvania Avenue, NW, #821
  Washington, DC 20006-1811
  Tel: 800-676-3685
  E-mail: adfboard@dispatcher.org
  http://www.dispatcher.org/

For information on aviation careers, contact
  Federal Aviation Administration
  800 Independence Avenue, SW
  Washington, DC 20591-0001
  Tel: 866-835-5322
  http://www.faa.gov/careers

Airport
Security Personnel

QUICK FACTS

School Subjects
Computer science
Government
Mathematics

Personal Skills
Following instructions
Leadership/management

Work Environment
Indoors and outdoors
Primarily multiple locations

Minimum Education Level
Some postsecondary training

Salary Range
$25,000 to $50,000 to
$150,000+

Certification or Licensing
None available

Outlook
Faster than the average

DOT
372

GOE
04.03.03

NOC
6651

O*NET-SOC
33-9032.00

OVERVIEW

Airport security personnel is a blanket term describing all workers who protect the safety of passengers and staff in the nation's airports and aircraft. One of the largest group of personnel in this line of work is *security screeners*, who are responsible for identifying dangerous objects or hazardous materials in baggage, cargo, or on traveling passengers and preventing these objects and their carriers from boarding planes. Also included in this group of workers are *air marshals*, who act as onboard security agents, protecting passengers, pilots, and other airline staff in the case of any emergencies while in the air. *Security directors* oversee security operations and staff for entire airports. More than 40,000 people are employed in airport security.

HISTORY

The use of screening and onboard security personnel is not a recent invention. The presence of guards on airplanes originated in the 1960s as a result of a number of hijackings of U.S. planes flying to and from Cuba. These guards, referred to as sky marshals, grew in number during the 1970s and then declined in later years with the lower occurrences of airplane hijackings. Airplane security staffing reached several thousand workers at the peak of this hijacking scare, and then dropped to fewer than 100 workers nationwide during its quietest times.

The 2001 terrorist attacks on the World Trade Center and the Pentagon spurred many changes in the realm of airport security.

Most notably, a new federal agency was born: the Transportation Security Administration (TSA), responsible for overseeing all security at the nation's airports. This agency made airport and airline security a federal responsibility, and as a result, all airport security personnel became federal employees. This was no small task. Previously, security screening in airports was handled by private security firms. These firms were inconsistent in their hiring and training methods and paid relatively low wages—resulting in high job turnover rates and inadequate screening of potentially dangerous objects and materials. With the shift of responsibility into the government's hands, standard training and hiring requirements were put in place. In addition to better screening, hiring, and training methods, the technology for screening bags and passengers has improved, increasing the chances that dangerous cargo and on-person threats can be located and prevented from boarding a plane.

THE JOB

Protecting U.S. skies, airports, and passengers is a huge undertaking that requires many qualified, well-trained individuals in different security roles. The most visible airport security worker is the security screener, also called the *baggage and passenger screener.* These workers use computers, X-ray machines, and handheld scanners to screen bags and their owners passing through airport terminals. In addition to using technology to help them identify dangerous items, they also have to depend on their own eyesight to catch suspicious behavior and read the X-ray screens for signs of danger. These workers must be focused and alert, while also remaining personable and courteous to people being screened. The screening process can take a lot of time during high-volume travel days, and passengers waiting in line may be late for a flight, impatient, or simply rude. For this reason, security screeners must be people-oriented, able to manage crowds, and maintain composure in what can be stressful conditions.

Did You Know?

In 2008, the TSA conducted an Organizational Satisfaction Survey of its workers. Ninety-four percent said that they believed their work was important, 82 percent said that they liked their jobs, and 78 percent planned to stay with the TSA for at least the next year.

The need for security is not limited to the ground. Air marshals, also called *security agents,* have the demanding job of protecting airline passengers and staff from onboard threats, such as terrorists, hijackers, bombs, or other weapons. These workers are often covert in their operations, meaning they may be dressed and seated like an

Airport security workers view security monitors, keeping an eye out for any suspicious activity. (*K. Brenninger, SV-Bilderdienst/The Image Works*)

average passenger to be able to watch for suspicious behavior and surprise a potential attacker. Much of the details of air marshal jobs are classified to protect national security, such as their exact number and identities, routes, and training procedures. However the basics of their job is much like that of a Secret Service agent. They must be attentive to all activity that goes on around them, identify potential threats to security, and deal with dangerous individuals or objects once exposed onboard. The main difference between air marshals and other security agents is they must be trained and able to handle possible warfare in a confined space at 30,000 feet in the air.

Another airport security job of high importance is that of *security director*. These workers, hired by the federal government, are responsible for all security personnel within an airport. They oversee the hiring, training, and work of baggage and passenger screeners, air marshals, and other security guards. In the nation's largest airports, such as JFK in New York City or O'Hare in Chicago, directors are in charge of hundreds of workers. Because of the high level of responsibility held by these workers, security directors often have previous experience in crisis management or law enforcement, such as police chiefs or military officers.

REQUIREMENTS
High School
To work in most airport security jobs, you should have at least a high school diploma. However, security screeners can sidestep this educational requirement with previous job experience in security. While in high school, take classes in history and government to familiarize yourself with previous events and political threats that have threatened our national security, such as foreign hijackers and terrorist operations. You should also be comfortable working with computers since most jobs in security involve a great deal of technology. Math classes can be beneficial because as a security worker, you must be analytical and observant to identify and catch dangers before they happen.

Postsecondary Training
All security workers, from screeners to directors, are highly trained before starting their jobs. Screeners are trained on how to operate and identify dangerous objects from the X-ray machines and handheld wands. They also must be prepared to manage potentially dangerous individuals. Screeners currently receive 40 hours of training before their first day at work, and receive an additional 60 hours of training while on the job. This training period may be extended due to increased

scrutiny on screeners' performance and heightened national security risks.

Air marshals are rigorously trained in classified training centers across the country, and they come to the job with previous on-the-job experience from serving in a military or civilian police force. Similarly, security directors must have previous federal security experience and are trained for up to 400 hours before taking on the responsibility of directing an entire airport security staff.

Other Requirements

All airport security personnel have demanding jobs that require a calm demeanor when under pressure. Screeners often have to stand for hours at a time and assist in lifting passengers' luggage onto the screening belt. Their eyesight must be strong enough to detect even the smallest of possible threats displayed on a computer screen. To ensure that individuals can handle these demands, potential screeners face many physical and vision tests to ensure they are up to the job. All screeners must be U.S. citizens or nationals and pass tests evaluating mental abilities (English reading, writing, and speaking), visual observation (including color perception), hearing, and manual dexterity. Similarly, air marshals and directors of security must pass vision and hearing tests and be in good physical shape to face and dominate potential attackers.

EXPLORING

To explore this job, observe security personnel at work your next time at the airport. Notice how many people are involved in screening luggage and passengers. While you should not talk to these screeners and other security staff while they are at work, you may be able to schedule an interview with security personnel while they are on break or perhaps over the phone. Talk to a teacher or your counselor for help in arranging this.

You can also learn about security jobs at your local library or online. Explore the Web sites of the Federal Aviation Administration (http://www.faa.gov) and the TSA (http://www.tsa.gov) for facts and job descriptions, changes in policy, and even summer camp opportunities.

EMPLOYERS

In late 2001, airport and airline security was placed under the oversight of the federal government. While some screening jobs may still be handled by private companies, all security personnel are screened and trained under federal rules and regulations. This shift in responsibility was done to improve standards in security and ensure the safety of U.S. passengers and airline staff. The TSA and the Federal Aviation Administration (FAA) are the employers of all airport security staff. There are more than 40,000 people employed in airport security.

STARTING OUT

Depending on the security level you want to be employed in, you can start out working with no more than a high school diploma and on-the-job training. Security screening jobs are a great way to start out in this line of work. These jobs provide front-line experience in airport security and can offer flexible part-time schedules.

Positions as air marshals or directors of security are not entry-level positions. If you are interested in one of these jobs, you will need previous experience with the police, U.S. military, or other position in which you have gained skills in protecting the lives of others.

ADVANCEMENT

Screening jobs have high turnover rates and, as a result, offer many chances for advancement. After a couple of years of experience in baggage and passenger screening, you can work into higher positions in management or busier traffic responsibility. Security managers may be responsible for hundreds of workers and oversee the hiring and training of new workers.

Positions as air marshals already offer a high level of responsibility, but qualified and talented individuals can advance into manager and director roles, responsible for hundreds and even thousands of workers.

EARNINGS

Before airline security was adopted by the TSA, screeners were paid minimum wage. But to attract and retain qualified and dedicated workers, earnings have been raised considerably, with most full-time screeners earning starting salaries of $25,000 to $36,000 a year. Their pay rises as their level of experience and responsibility increases. Experienced screeners can earn up to $50,000 annually. Air marshals and directors earn much more, with directors topping out at a salary of $150,000 or more—one of the highest salaries in government service.

Benefits include paid vacation, health, disability, life insurance, and retirement or pension plans.

WORK ENVIRONMENT

As previously stated, any job in airport security is demanding and stressful, especially during high periods of travel, such as the holidays. Screeners face physical challenges of standing, bending, and lifting during their shifts, while having to maintain total visual focus on their X-ray machines or while searching individual passengers by hand.

The job of air marshals can be extremely stressful. These workers must be prepared to overcome an attacker in a confined space without risking harm to any of the plane's passengers. In addition, air marshals must spend considerable time away from home.

OUTLOOK

With the new awareness of airline dangers following recent terrorist attacks, the employment of airport security personnel will grow at a faster than average rate. Despite better pay, security screeners still have high turnover rates due to the high demands involved with the job. This turnover will continue to create many new jobs in the future. While jobs as air marshals and security directors will not be as plentiful, there will always be a critical need for qualified and skilled individuals to protect airplanes and passengers from security threats.

FOR MORE INFORMATION

The FAA offers a wealth of information on its Web site, from airline accident statistics and career guidance to information on summer camps for middle and high school students interested in aviation careers.

Federal Aviation Administration (FAA)
800 Independence Avenue, SW
Washington, DC 20591-0001
Tel: 866-835-5322
http://www.faa.gov

According to its Web site, the TSA "sets the standard for excellence in transportation security through its people, processes, and technologies." Explore the site for details on the nation's threat advisory level and tips on flying and packing safely.

Transportation Security Administration (TSA)
Office of Law Enforcement-Federal Air Marshal Service
601 South 12th Street
Arlington, VA 20598-0100
http://www.tsa.gov

Airport
Service Workers

OVERVIEW

The term *airport service worker* is a general designation for a wide variety of workers who are employed in support occupations at airports. Many of these workers deal directly with the public in sales- and service-based occupations. Others perform behind-the-scenes maintenance and cleaning services that keep public and private areas of airports clean and operating efficiently.

HISTORY

In the early days of aviation, there were no airports as we know them today. Planes landed on flat strips of dirt and grass, and there were few, if any, services available for passengers. By the 1930s, the first airports were constructed in New York, Chicago, and other major cities. But it was not until after World War II that commercial air travel began to really take off and services began to be offered to make travel easier and more convenient for airline passengers. Large numbers of airport service workers were hired to staff airport restaurants and shops, keep facilities clean, and assist travelers with baggage and general information. Today, these workers serve more than 30 million travelers annually at approximately 517 commercial services airports in the United States.

QUICK FACTS

(continued)

O*NET-SOC
11-9051.00, 35-1011.00,
35-1012.00, 35-2011.00,
35-2014.00, 35-2015.00,
35-2021.00, 35-3011.00,
35-3021.00, 35-3022.00,
35-3031.00, 35-9011.00,
35-9021.00, 37-1011.02,
37-1012.00, 37-2011.00,
37-3011.00, 39-6011.00,
39-6032.00, 41-1011.00,
41-2011.00, 41-2031.00,
53-6021.00

THE JOB

Airport service workers perform a variety of duties that are integral to the proper functioning of an airport. The following paragraphs detail some of the major airport service careers.

Airport parking attendants sell parking tickets, collect payments, and direct cars into the proper parking spaces. Many airports offer transportation from remote parking lots to the terminals. *Airport drivers* operate trolley cars, trams, buses, vans, and trains and give general assistance to passengers. Some airport drivers operate airfield vehicles such as food trucks, employee buses, fuel trucks, and other equipment.

Skycaps, also known as *baggage porters*, help customers with luggage at airports. They are either employed by airlines or by ground services companies. Skycaps stand at curbside airline entrances and help travelers load and unload baggage, answer questions about flight schedules, and often check in luggage.

Airport concession workers are employed at gift shops, bookstores, car rental agencies, newsstands, and any other place goods or services are sold. Besides making and completing cash and credit card sales, attendants are responsible for stocking and pricing items, helping customers with their purchases, and answering any questions regarding the merchandise or services. Attendants also make sure displays are clean and orderly.

Airport food concession attendants sell snacks and beverages to travelers at small airport kiosks. Attendants are trained on the proper way to prepare and serve their snacks and make cash and credit card transactions as well.

Airport food service workers are employed in eating establishments at airports. *Waiters* and *waitresses* take customers' orders, serve food and beverages, calculate bills, and sometimes collect money. Between serving customers, waiters and waitresses may clear and clean tables and counters, replenish supplies, and set up table service for future customers. *Cooks* and *chefs* are employed in the preparation and cooking of food in restaurants and other eating establishments. *Fast food workers* take food and drink orders from customers. During quiet periods, they may be responsible for such chores as making coffee, cooking French fries, or cleaning tables. *Bartenders* mix and dispense alcoholic and nonalcoholic drinks in airport restaurants and bars.

Restaurant and food service managers are responsible for the overall operation of airport businesses that serve food. Food service work includes the purchasing of a variety of food, selection of the menu, preparation of the food, and, most importantly, maintenance of health and sanitation levels. It is the responsibility of managers to oversee staffing for each task in addition to performing the business and accounting functions of restaurant operations.

Some airport food service workers are employed by the airlines or private contractors to prepare and cook food that is consumed during flights. They work in airport flight kitchens. Other food service employees in airports include bar backs, buspersons, dishwashers, and kitchen assistants.

Airport janitors or cleaners clean and maintain all areas of the airport, including terminals, washrooms, security areas, shops, restaurants, bars, waiting areas, and offices. In addition to daily cleaning duties, they may perform light repair work when needed and make sure heating and cooling systems are in proper working order. Larger airports employ separate tradesworkers, such as carpenters, electricians, plumbers, and building engineers, to repair and maintain airport facilities.

Groundsmanagers and *groundskeepers* oversee the maintenance of land and vegetation at airports and their surrounding facilities.

Airport information specialists assist passengers in airport terminals. They answer general questions and help disabled passengers. Some airport information specialists work as *translators* and help foreign travelers.

REQUIREMENTS

High School

While most airport service positions are available to high school students, the most attractive positions will go to high school graduates. In high school, take courses in mathematics, business, and computer science to prepare for work in these careers. English and speech classes will help you to develop your communication skills, and a foreign language will help you to interact with foreign travelers.

Postsecondary Training

Most airport service positions are open to high school students. They learn the duties and responsibilities of their specific position via on-the-job training. Other airport service workers prepare for their careers by enrolling in postsecondary training programs. For example, cooks and chefs may pursue additional education at private vocational schools or university programs. They may also participate in apprenticeship programs that are sponsored by professional associations and trade unions. To improve their management abilities and increase their chances of promotion, many food service managers earn an associate's or bachelor's degree in restaurant management or institutional food service management. Airport tradesworkers, such as carpenters, electricians, plumbers, and building engineers, usually learn their respective trade by participating in an apprenticeship program or attending a technical or vocational educational program.

Certification or Licensing

Certification and licensing requirements vary based on the type of airport service career. The following paragraphs detail certification and licensing requirements for selected airport service careers.

Applicants who pass an examination can receive the certified parking professional designation from the National Parking Association.

In most states, airport and other professional drivers must qualify for a commercial driver's license. State motor vehicle departments can provide information on how to qualify for this license. For insurance reasons, companies generally prefer to hire drivers who are at least 25 years of age and have an impeccable driving record.

Chefs, cooks, and other food service workers are required by law in most states to possess a health certificate and to be examined periodically. These examinations, usually given by the state board of health, make certain that the individual is free from communicable diseases and skin infections. The National Restaurant Association Educational Foundation offers a voluntary foodservice management professional certification to restaurant and food service managers.

Although not a requirement for finding a job, some janitors opt to become certified by the National Executive Housekeepers Association.

Groundsmanagers and groundskeepers can receive voluntary certification from several organizations, including the Professional Landcare Network and the Professional Grounds Management Society.

Other Requirements

Airport service workers who deal with the public must have strong communication skills, pleasant personal appearances, tact, patience, and the ability to interact with a wide range of people. All workers must be able to follow instructions and have good physical stamina to stand for long periods of time. Workers who are employed in sales

Facts About the Airline Industry

- U.S. and Canadian airlines operate more than 8,000 aircraft.
- More than two billion passengers travel by airplane worldwide each year.
- Approximately 487,000 people were employed in the U.S. air transportation industry in 2006.
- There are 517 commercial service airports in the United States.

Sources: Air Line Pilots Association, International

occupations must be able to add and subtract accurately and quickly and operate cash registers and other types of business machines.

Skycaps must have physical strength to lift heavy luggage and excellent communication skills to deal with customers effectively. Airport drivers must have a good driving record and be able drive in all types of weather conditions.

Bartenders must be at least 21 years of age, although some employers prefer they be older than 25. In some states, bartenders must have health certificates assuring that they are free of contagious diseases. Because of the large sums of money collected in some bars, bartenders must sometimes be bonded.

Janitors and tradesworkers should be good with their hands and be able to operate tools and equipment. A certain level of stamina and energy is essential since the job requires physical labor.

Groundskeepers must be able to follow directions and be responsible, since they are often assigned duties and then asked to work without direct supervision.

Information specialists must have excellent communication skills and an encyclopedic knowledge of airport services and facilities in order to quickly and effectively serve the needs of travelers.

EXPLORING

One way to learn more about these careers is to visit an airport and watch these workers as they do their jobs. You might also ask your counselor or teacher to set up an information interview with a worker in the field. You can also try to get a part-time or summer job at an airport as a food service worker, shop clerk, janitor, information specialist, or other service worker.

EMPLOYERS

Airport service workers are employed at the approximately 517 commercial services airports in the United States. Some work directly for airlines, while others work for private contractors. Additionally, almost all of these positions can be found outside of airports. For example, skycaps are also employed in bus terminals, train stations, cruise ships, and just about any place of travel. Skycaps known as *baggage porters* and *bellhops* assist guests at hotels and motels. Food service workers are employed by hotels, bars, restaurants, and schools. Janitors and cleaners work in hotels, restaurants, offices, schools, malls, stadiums, and in countless other settings. Grounds workers are employed at golf and country clubs, public parks and recreation areas, apartment complexes, cemeteries, condominiums, estates, schools and universities, shopping centers and malls, theme parks, zoos, commercial and industrial parks, hospitals, and military installations. Information specialists can also be employed at rail and bus stations, amusement parks, shopping malls, trade shows, concert halls, and sports stadiums.

STARTING OUT

Airport service careers represent an excellent way to break into the aviation industry at the ground level. Contact your local airport authority for a list of concession contractors to which you can apply for employment directly.

ADVANCEMENT

With hard work, dedication, and additional education or training, airport service workers can advance to a variety of managerial and supervisory positions. For example, food service workers can become chefs or food service managers. Experienced janitors and cleaners may be asked to supervise large groups of workers. Those with experience, contacts, references, and an interest in entrepreneurship could start their own businesses.

EARNINGS

Salaries for airport service workers vary based on the size and location of the airport and the worker's job description and level of experience. Airport drivers earn approximately $7 to $8 an hour. Skycaps earn salaries that range from $13,200 to $25,200 plus tips, according to the Federal Aviation Administration (FAA). According to CNN.com, experienced skycaps can earn between $75,000 and

$100,000 a year. Airport concession workers earn salaries that range from minimum wage to approximately $10 per hour. Food preparers earn $6 to $10 an hour. Food service managers earned median annual salaries of $46,320 in 2008, according to the U.S. Department of Labor. Janitors and cleaners had median annual salaries of $21,450 in 2008.

Benefits for full-time workers include vacation and sick time, health, and sometimes dental, insurance, and pension or 401(k) plans.

WORK ENVIRONMENT

With millions of travelers from countless states and countries passing through annually, airports are hectic but exciting places to work. And like the diverse travelers they serve, airport service workers enjoy a wide variety of work environments. Workers employed in concessions and food service work indoors in a comfortable, climate-controlled environment. Others, such as janitors and cleaners and maintenance staff, work both indoors and outdoors to keep airport facilities maintained. Skycaps spend most of their workday outdoors on their feet in sometimes severe weather conditions. Airport drivers work in all types of weather conditions. They are constantly on the go, transporting passengers, airport employees, and equipment and goods to various locations. Groundsmanagers and groundskeeping crews work outside year-round in all types and conditions of weather. Grounds workers frequently use pesticides, herbicides, and fungicides to keep turf, plants, shrubs, trees, and flowers healthy and beautiful. It is essential that they observe safety precautions when applying these chemicals to prevent exposure.

Since most airports are open 24 hours a day, seven days a week, airport service workers may be required to work nights and on weekends.

OUTLOOK

Employment in the air transportation industry is expected to grow about as fast as the average for all industries through 2018, according to the *Career Guide to Industries*. As a result of reduced passenger travel in recent years, there have been many layoffs and some airlines and other aviation-related companies went bankrupt. The U.S. Department of Labor predicts that the industry will gradually recover as the economy improves and world trade expands.

The threat of terrorism has a large effect on the employment of airport service workers. Another terrorist attack or even the threat of an attack will greatly affect the employment of airport service workers. If the public travels less, there will be less demand for service and support workers at airports. Certain positions will be hit especially hard. For example, during heightened security alerts, curbside check-in is banned, which affects employment for skycaps.

Overall, there should be many job openings for workers in this field since these positions pay relatively low salaries and require little educational preparation. Positions will become available as workers leave the field for better-paying positions with more opportunity for advancement.

FOR MORE INFORMATION

To read The Airline Handbook, *visit the ATAA Web site.*
   Air Transport Association of America (ATAA)
   1301 Pennsylvania Avenue, NW, Suite 1100
   Washington, DC 20004-1738
   Tel: 202-626-4000
   E-mail: ata@airlines.org
   http://www.airlines.org

For information on careers and training in the janitorial services field, contact
   Cleaning and Maintenance Management Online
   National Trade Publications
   19 British American Boulevard West
   Latham, NY 12110-6405
   Tel: 518-783-1281
   http://www.cmmonline.com

For general information on aviation, contact
   Federal Aviation Administration
   800 Independence Avenue, SW
   Washington, DC 20591
   Tel: 202-366-4000
   http://www.faa.gov

For information on educational programs, contact
   International Council on Hotel, Restaurant and Institutional Education
   2810 North Parham Road, Suite 230
   Richmond, VA 23294-4422
   Tel: 804-346-4800
   http://chrie.org

For information about certification programs in housekeeping, contact
International Executive Housekeepers Association
1001 Eastwind Drive, Suite 301
Westerville, OH 43081-3361
Tel: 800-200-6342
E-mail: excel@ieha.org
http://www.ieha.org

For information on certification for parking facility managers, contact
National Parking Association
1112 16th Street, NW, Suite 840
Washington, DC 20036-4816
Tel: 800-647-7275
E-mail: info@npapark.org
http://www.npapark.org

For information on education, scholarships, and careers, contact
National Restaurant Association Educational Foundation
175 West Jackson Boulevard, Suite 1500
Chicago, IL 60604-2702
Tel: 800-765-2122
E-mail: info@restaurant.org
http://www.nraef.org

For materials on educational programs and careers in the retail industry, contact
National Retail Federation
325 7th Street, NW, Suite 1100
Washington, DC 20004-2825
Tel: 800-673-4692
http://www.nrf.com

For information on certification, contact
Professional Grounds Management Society
720 Light Street
Baltimore, MD 21230-3850
Tel: 410-223-2861
E-mail: pgms@assnhqtrs.com
http://www.pgms.org

Air Traffic Controllers

QUICK FACTS

School Subjects
Computer science
Geography

Personal Skills
Leadership/management
Technical/scientific

Work Environment
Primarily indoors
Primarily one location

Minimum Education Level
Bachelor's degree

Salary Range
$33,700 to $111,870 to
$200,000+

Certification or Licensing
Required by all states

Outlook
About as fast as the average

DOT
193

GOE
07.02.01

NOC
2272

O*NET-SOC
53-2021.00

OVERVIEW

Air traffic controllers monitor and direct the activities of aircraft into and out of airports and along specified flight routes. They radio pilots with approach, landing, taxiing, and takeoff instructions and advisories on weather and other conditions in order to maintain the safe and orderly flow of air traffic both in the air and on the ground. There are approximately 26,200 air traffic controllers employed in the United States.

HISTORY

The goal of the first air traffic control efforts—beacon lights—was to guide airplanes along a specified airway. As airways and aircraft grew in number, radio communication and radio beacons were added to help planes navigate and to provide weather forecasts. In 1936, the federal government opened the first air traffic control center to regulate the increasing numbers of aircraft flying into and out of the country's growing airports. The Instrument Landing System, a method for signaling aircraft, was instituted in 1941. Airplanes were reaching higher speeds and altitudes, and the controllers' functions became more important to guard against collisions, to ensure safe landings, and to warn pilots of potential weather and geographic hazards in flights. Radar, developed during World War II, allowed air traffic controllers to track the movements of many aircraft and for longer distances. The air traffic control network was extended to include centers at airports, en route centers, and flight service stations, each of which performed specific tasks and controlled specific portions of the skies. After the war, more sophisticated communication systems were developed, including VOR (very high frequency omnidirectional range) transmission, which was used to signal flight path data directly to the plane. Computers were soon installed in order to provide still greater accuracy to the air traffic controller's instructions. Development of the Global Positioning System (GPS), however, has made it possible for airplanes to achieve greater control over their flight paths, so fewer air traffic controllers will be needed to protect the skies.

THE JOB

Air traffic controllers work in one of three areas: airport traffic control towers, en route air traffic control centers, or flight service stations. The Federal Aviation Administration (FAA), which regulates all air traffic, employs almost every air traffic controller in the United States. Some private airports employ their own air traffic controllers; others are employed at military airports.

Terminal air traffic control specialists are stationed in airport control towers and are responsible for all air traffic entering, leaving, or passing through the airspace around the airport, as well as conducting airplane traffic on the ground. These controllers use radar and visual observation to maintain safe distances among aircraft, and they provide information on weather and other conditions to the pilots under their control. As an airplane prepares for departure, the *ground controller* issues taxiing instructions to bring it to the runway. A *local controller* contacts the pilot with weather, wind, speed, and visibility conditions and clears the pilot for takeoff. A *departure controller* monitors the aircraft on radar, maintains radio contact with the pilot until the aircraft has left the airport's airspace, and hands over control of the plane to an en route control center. A *radar controller* monitors the traffic above the airport and into the aircraft's flight route, communicating with the other controllers. Approaching aircraft are handled in a reverse procedure. When many aircraft are approaching the airport at the same time, the controllers arrange them in a holding pattern above the airport until they each can be cleared to land.

There are more than 440 air traffic control towers in airports across the country. At a small airport, an air traffic controller may be expected to perform all of these functions. Controllers at larger airports usually specialize in a single area. *Senior controllers* supervise the activities of the entire center. Terminal air traffic controllers may be responsible for all aircraft within as much as a 50-mile radius of their airport. Most controllers are responsible for many aircraft at once; they track their positions on the radar screen, receive instrument flight data such as an airplane's speed and altitude, coordinate the altitudes at which planes within the area will fly, keep track of weather conditions, and maintain constant communication with the pilots and with controllers at their and other control centers. An air traffic controller must be aware of all of the activities in the air traffic control center and around the airport. When an aircraft experiences an emergency, air traffic controllers must respond quickly, clearing a path for that aircraft through the traffic, alerting fire and rescue teams, and guiding the pilot to a safe landing.

En route air traffic control specialists work at one of 21 regional centers in the United States. They coordinate the movements of aircraft between airports but out of range of the airport traffic controllers. Because an en route center may be responsible for many thousands of square miles of airspace, these controllers generally work in teams of two or three, with each team assigned a particular section of the center's airspace. Each team consists of a radar controller, the senior member of the team, and radar associates. A center may employ as many as 700 controllers and have 150 or more on duty during peak flying hours. Within the center's airspace are designated routes that the aircraft fly. En route controllers monitor traffic along those air routes. They use radar and electronic equipment to track the flights within the center's airspace and to maintain contact with planes within their area, giving instructions, air traffic clearances, and advice about flight conditions. If flight plans for two airplanes conflict, the en route team will contact the team responsible for the preceding section in order to change one plane's flight path. The controllers will also coordinate changes in altitudes and speeds among pilots. En route controllers receive or transfer control of the aircraft to controllers in adjacent centers or to an airport's approach controller as the craft enters that facility's airspace.

Flight service station air traffic control specialists make up the third group of controllers. They provide pre-flight or in-flight assistance to pilots from more than 125 flight service stations linked by a broad communications system. These controllers give pilots information about the station's particular area, including terrain, weather, and anything else necessary to guarantee a safe flight. They may suggest alternate routes or different altitudes, alert pilots to military operations taking place along certain routes, inform them about landing at airports that have no towers, assist pilots in emergency situations, and participate in searches for missing or overdue aircraft.

REQUIREMENTS

High School

Because it is highly recommended for all air traffic controllers to have a college degree, high school students interested in the field will be best prepared by pursuing a college prep curriculum. Mathematics and science courses are especially useful courses to study because they are most directly related to air traffic control work.

Postsecondary Training

To become an air traffic controller, a person must enroll in an education program recognized by the FAA. (Visit http://www.faa.gov/jobs/job_opportunities/airtraffic_controllers for a list of schools.) They must also pass a pre-employment test that gauges their aptitude for the career and have completed four years of college or have three years of work experience or a combination of both. Entry to civil aviation is also possible through the military.

Those accepted into the training program receive 12 weeks of intensive instruction at the FAA Academy in Oklahoma City. There they receive training in the fundamentals of the airway systems, civil air regulations, radar, and aircraft performance characteristics. They practice on machines designed to simulate emergency situations to determine their emotional stability under pressure. The standards for those who successfully complete this program are very high; about 50 percent of the trainees are dropped during this period. Those who complete the program are guaranteed jobs with the FAA.

Certification or Licensing

Training continues on the job, and new controllers also receive classroom instruction. Depending on the size and complexity of the facility, a new hire may require between 24 and 48 months to become a fully certified air traffic controller. Controllers must be certified at each progressive level of air traffic control, usually within a certain period of time. Failure to be certified within the time limit is grounds for dismissal. Air traffic controllers are also required to pass annual physical exams and performance reviews.

Other Requirements

Applicants for airport tower or en route traffic control jobs must be 30 years of age or younger, pass physical and psychological examinations, be U.S. citizens, and have vision that is or can be corrected to 20/20. Flight service stations will accept applicants who are over the age of 30. Those hoping to enter the field must be articulate, have

A tower controller provides landing instructions to an incoming jet. (*National Air Traffic Controllers Association*)

a good memory, and show self-control. It is imperative that they be able to express themselves clearly, remember rapidly changing data that affect their decisions, and be able to operate calmly under very difficult situations involving a great deal of strain. They must also be able to make good, sound, and quickly derived decisions. A poor decision may mean the loss of a large number of lives.

EXPLORING

If you are interested in this career, you can begin exploring by arranging for a visit to an air traffic control center. Many centers welcome and encourage such visits. Talking with air traffic controllers and watching them work will provide you with a strong introduction to their day-to-day activities. Speaking with aircraft pilots may provide other insights into the role of the air traffic controller. Visits and interviews can be arranged through most airports, air traffic control centers, the Air Traffic Control Association, and many airlines. You should also be aware that every branch of the military offers opportunities for experience in these and related jobs.

EMPLOYERS

Air traffic controllers are employed by the federal government. Most work for the FAA, although a small number work in such areas as the Department of Defense. Approximately 26,200 air traffic controllers work in the United States.

STARTING OUT

The first step in becoming an air traffic controller starts with the written civil service exam, followed by the one-week screening. Acceptance is on a highly competitive basis. High grades in college or strong work experience is considered essential. Experience in related fields, including those of pilots, air dispatch operators, and other positions with either the civil airlines or the military service, will be important for those with and especially for those without a college degree. Actual air control experience gained in military service may be a plus. However, civil aviation rules are quite different from military aviation rules. Because the FAA provides complete training, applicants with strong skills and abilities in abstract reasoning, communication, and problem solving, as well as the ability to learn and to work independently, will have the best chance of entering this field.

ADVANCEMENT

After becoming a controller, those who do particularly well may reach the level of supervisor or manager. Many others advance to even more responsible positions in air control, and some might move into the top administrative jobs with the FAA. Competitive civil service status can be earned at the end of one year on the job, and career status after the satisfactory completion of three years of work in the area.

In the case of both airport control specialists and en route control specialists, the responsibilities become more complex with each successive promotion. Controllers generally begin at the GS-7 level and advance by completing certification requirements for the different air traffic control specialists. New hires at an airport control tower usually begin by communicating flight data and airport conditions to pilots before progressing through the ranks of ground controller, local controller, departure controller, and, lastly, arrival controller. At an en route center, trainees begin by processing flight plans, then advance to become radar associate controllers, and, finally, radar controllers.

After becoming fully qualified, controllers who exhibit strong management, organizational, and job skills may advance to become area supervisors and managers and control tower or flight service station managers. Employees in the higher grades may be responsible for a number of different areas, including the coordination of the traffic control activities within the control area, the supervision and training of en route traffic controllers or airport traffic controllers in lower positions, and management in various aeronautical agencies. These positions generally become available after three to five years of fully qualified service.

EARNINGS

Air traffic control trainees earn starting salaries of about $33,700. This pay level increases as workers gain experience and meet training goals. According to the U.S. Department of Labor, in 2008 the average salary for air traffic controllers in nonsupervisory, supervisory, and managerial jobs was $111,870. The lowest paid 10 percent of controllers made less than $45,020. The highest paid controllers made $161,010 or more per year. The controller's experience, job responsibilities, and the complexity of the facility are also factors that influence the rate of pay. Controllers with a great deal of seniority and those at the nation's busiest airports can earn more than $200,000 per year in wages, overtime, and benefits. Controllers may also earn bonuses based on performance.

Because of the complexity of their job duties and the tension involved in their work, air traffic controllers are offered better benefits than other federal employees. Depending on their length of service, air traffic controllers receive 13 to 26 days of paid vacation and 13 days of paid sick leave per year, plus life insurance and health benefits. In addition, they are permitted to retire earlier and with fewer years of service than other federal employees. An air traffic controller with 20 years of experience may retire at the age of 50; those with 25 years of experience may retire at any age. Controllers who manage air traffic are required to retire at age 56. Air traffic controllers who have top skills and experience can receive a retirement exemption up to age 61.

WORK ENVIRONMENT

Air traffic controllers are required to remain constantly alert and focused while performing a large number of simultaneous duties. They must keep track of several aircraft approaching, departing, and passing through the airspace under their control, while receiving flight data from and giving instructions to several pilots at once. They must remain alert to changes in weather and airport conditions, guide planes through intricate approach patterns, and maintain a safe separation of aircraft in the sky and on the ground. They must be able to interpret the symbols on the radar screen, form a clear image of what is happening in the sky above them, and react quickly and decisively to the activity of the aircraft. Controllers must also have strong communicative abilities and be able to give instructions to pilots in a firm and clear tone. The stress of the controller's job requires a great deal of emotional control, especially in times of potential danger and emergency. Traffic conditions change continuously throughout the controller's shift, and the controller must remain alert during times of light traffic as well as times of heavy traffic.

Terminal air traffic controllers work in towers as high as 200 feet off the ground; windows on all sides of the tower allow the pilot to see what is happening on the runways and in the sky around the airport. Radar control screens provide locations of all aircraft in the airport's airspace. Large air traffic control towers generally house the radar control center in a room below the observation tower. En route centers are usually housed in large, windowless buildings. These controllers monitor the sky entirely through radar and radio communication. Flight service stations are often located at airports in separate buildings from the control tower.

The numbers of air traffic controllers on duty varies from airport to airport and according to the number of scheduled flights expected in a center's airspace. At a small airport, a controller may work alone for an entire shift; larger airports may have up to 30 controllers on duty, while en route centers may have more than 150 controllers on duty during a shift. Air traffic controllers work a five-day, 40-hour week, usually on a rotating shift basis, which means they often work at night, during the weekends, and during holidays. Overtime is often available; during a shift, controllers are given breaks every two hours.

OUTLOOK

There are two schools of thought regarding the employment outlook for air traffic controllers. The U.S. Department of Labor predicts growth about as fast as the average for all occupations through 2018 as a result of strong and continued competition for air traffic control positions, and the implementation of a new air traffic control system that will reduce employment for workers in the field. On the other hand, the National Air Traffic Controllers Association predicts that employment opportunities will be good over the next seven to eight years as half of the nation's controllers near retirement age. Additionally, the FAA anticipates that it will need to hire 17,000 new workers by 2017. Many industry experts dispute these predictions, arguing that many controllers will stay on after they become eligible for retirement because of good pay and benefits.

Whatever their employment outlook, it is clear that the role of the air traffic controller has begun to change. More and more planes are being equipped with GPS technology. GPS allows planes to form a far more accurate picture of their position and the position of others in the sky. This allows planes to break away from the traditional air routes and essentially chart their own course, allowing for faster and more economical flights. These developments may limit employment opportunities for air traffic controllers. Openings in the field will come primarily from retiring controllers and others who leave the job.

FOR MORE INFORMATION

For information on air traffic control and scholarships for college students, contact
Air Traffic Control Association
1101 King Street, Suite 300
Alexandria, VA 22314-2963
Tel: 703-299-2430
E-mail: info@atca.org
http://www.atca.org

For career information, contact
Federal Aviation Administration
800 Independence Avenue, SW
Washington, DC 20591-0001
Tel: 866-835-5322
http://jobs.faa.gov

For career and education information, contact
National Air Traffic Controllers Association
1325 Massachusetts Avenue, NW
Washington, DC 20005-4171
Tel: 202-628-5451
E-mail: web-staff@list.natca.net
http://www.natca.org

For information on air traffic control and industry publications, contact
National Association of Air Traffic Specialists
PO Box 2550
Landover Hills, MD 20784-0550
Tel: 301-459-5595

For information on air traffic control careers in Canada, contact the following associations:
Canadian Air Traffic Control Association
304 - 265 Carling Avenue
Ottawa, ON K1S 2E1 Canada
Tel: 613-225-8448
E-mail: catca@catca.ca
http://www.catca.ca

Nav Canada
PO Box 3411, Station D
Ottawa, ON K1P 5L6 Canada
Tel: 877-663-6656
http://www.navcanada.ca

INTERVIEW

Ann Marie Taggio is an air traffic controller at Charlotte-Douglas International Airport in Charlotte, North Carolina. She discussed her career with the editors of Careers in Focus: Aviation.

Q. What made you want to become an air traffic controller?

A. I discovered this career by accident. I had a friend whose husband was an air traffic controller—and he thought the world of his job. He wanted his wife to become an air traffic controller. When it came time to take the civil service test, he asked me to accompany her and take the test as well. I did really well on the test, scoring a 94 percent. From there, I went on to study at the Air Traffic Controller Academy.

Q. What type of training did you undertake to become an air traffic controller?

A. When I first entered this field, you needed to pass a civil service test and then go on to training from there. Part of this was because of the high need for air traffic controllers. Years later there was not as much of a pressing need. Many of the new hires came from an aviation background. However, many of the current controllers are coming up to retirement age, so again there is a pressing need for new hires. Many come with four-year degrees, from the military, as well as those from a civil background. Some airports may prefer that you have an aviation degree, but I feel you can be successful in this job if you are logical and able to think on your feet.

Q. What is a typical day like on the job?

A. On a clear day, I am responsible for 100 airplanes arriving and 100 airplanes departing. This doesn't count any airplanes flying through our airspace, or any private planes flying over asking for directions or assistance. When the weather is bad, we can count on lower levels of airplanes.

We are essentially cops in the air, as opposed to cops at an intersection directing traffic. We direct traffic in the air. I work five days a week, 40 hours a week. I start on Thursday and work from there. My shift starts at 3:00 P.M. and runs to 11:00 P.M. When I come to work, I am assigned a particular area. At Charlotte-Douglas International Airport, you may be assigned to work in the tower, the glass tower most people see at the airport, or at the base of the tower, which is called the radar room. You are responsible for your assigned position. During your break time, another person will take over your position, or you may be responsible for another controller's assignment during their off time. At Charlotte-Douglas International Airport, you are given permanent days on and off, which may mean weekend or holiday shifts.

When working in the tower, our job level depends on the weather. When the weather is bad, there are certain rules and regulations you have to follow. There may be more incidents where pilots ask for different altitudes—for example, higher or lower to get past a storm cloud or turbulence.

We use weather radar to help keep pilots away from bad weather. But sometimes you can't predict turbulence in the air, and rely on reports coming from the pilots. When we get such reports from pilots, we can then assume that more similar requests will be coming from pilots in the same area. Situations such as this may make our workloads more difficult. Experience will help you make such judgment calls.

Q. What is the most important quality needed for success in this career?

A. I think it's important to have a confident personality. This quality is needed because you must be able to make quick decisions. What's important to display while you are working is that you are in control of everything, even when something goes bad. You have to have the inner strength to know "I can do this."

Q. What is the future employment outlook for air traffic controllers?

A. The outlook is good, partly because of new technology and equipment used in the field. Also because many of those employed today are approaching the mandatory retirement age. There are many opportunities for women. When I first entered the field, it was very much male-dominated. That has changed. There are now many women working as air traffic controllers, some in management positions.

Q. What advice would you give to young people who want to enter the field?

A. You don't need to love airplanes for this job, but you do need to love action and a fast pace, which is part of the job.

I would advise students to take math and computer classes. If you want to explore the field, it would be a good idea to contact your local airport and schedule a tour of the facility. Many airports offer tours to school groups, but you may be able to schedule a tour simply by calling up and saying you want to learn more about the airport, specifically air traffic control.

Aviation
Safety Inspectors

QUICK FACTS

School Subjects
Mathematics
Physics

Personal Skills
Mechanical/manipulative
Technical/scientific

Work Environment
Indoors and outdoors
Primarily multiple locations

Minimum Education Level
High school diploma

Salary Range
$27,560 to $55,250 to
$101,010+

Certification or Licensing
Required for certain positions

Outlook
Faster than the average

DOT
168, 196, 621

GOE
04.04.02, 07.08.01,
08.02.03

NOC
2262

O*NET-SOC
51-9061.04, 53-6051.01

OVERVIEW

The regulations of the Federal Aviation Administration (FAA) are enforced by *aviation safety inspectors* who usually specialize in general aviation or commercial aircraft. They inspect maintenance, manufacturing, repair, and operations procedures and also certify pilots, flight instructors, flight examiners, repair facilities, and aviation schools. They are responsible for the quality and safety of aircraft equipment and personnel. Aviation safety inspectors are classified under the heading of transportation inspectors. There are approximately 26,000 *transportation inspectors* in the United States.

HISTORY

Although the U.S. Constitution gives Congress the power to regulate and control interstate travel via the highway, railway, and water, it does not mention anything about the air. Indeed, the framers of that document did not foresee the age of air travel that would begin in a little more than 100 years. The Wright brothers may have flown the first airplane in 1903, but air travel was not regulated until 1926 when the Secretary of Commerce was given the authority to create a regulatory system. This system was the precursor to the agencies that would later employ many aviation safety inspectors. The system evolved as much as it could to keep pace with the burgeoning field of air transportation until the 1950s, when it could no longer handle the rapidly occurring changes in the field and became outdated. To address these changes, the Federal Aviation Agency was created in 1958. The Federal Aviation Agency was given the authority to promote the development and safety of air transportation through regulations. One of its responsibilities is to set and enforce safety standards. It later became a part of the Department of Transportation (DOT) and was renamed the Federal Aviation Administration. Another government agency concerned with aviation safety, the National Transportation Safety Board (NTSB), was established in 1967 as a part of the DOT and was made an independent agency in 1975. The NTSB is responsible for investigating aviation accidents, determining the probable cause of accidents, and making recommendations for safety improvements in the field of aviation. Outside of the United States, the growing need for air safety issues and regulations was addressed by the creation of the International Civil Aviation Organization in 1944, and the International Air Transport Association in 1945.

THE JOB

The duties of an aviation safety inspector generally include making sure that aircraft are airworthy, that the facilities and equipment surrounding aircraft are safe, and that the personnel working on or flying aircraft complete their work safely and correctly. The specific duties of aviation safety inspectors depend on the area in which they specialize.

Aviation safety inspectors usually work in one of three general areas: operations, pertaining to the operation of aircraft; manufacturing, pertaining to the manufacture of aircraft or related equipment; or airworthiness, pertaining to the maintenance and repair of aircraft and related equipment in order to ensure safe flight. In addition, the FAA has identified and defined eight different types of aviation safety inspectors: *general aviation avionics inspectors, general aviation maintenance inspectors, general aviation operations inspectors, air carrier avionics inspectors, air carrier maintenance inspectors, air carrier operations inspectors, manufacturing inspectors,* and *cabin safety inspectors.* These inspectors all administer and enforce safety regulations and uphold set standards. The differences are in the general areas that the inspectors regulate and/or the size of the aircraft they inspect.

Aviation safety inspectors working in operations are concerned with the people operating aircraft and their training programs, equipment, and facilities. The inspector evaluates pilots, navigators, and flight instructors and issues initial certification that they are proficient and meet the necessary requirements. This certification is done on a continuing basis, and the inspector is responsible for that as well. They also evaluate the manner in which these workers are trained, the equipment they use, and the facilities in which they work and train to make sure they meet safety regulations and standards. One way an inspector might do this is by running simulations with flight personnel, ground crews, and air traffic controllers to monitor performance of the people and equipment involved.

Aviation safety inspectors working in manufacturing are concerned with the design and manufacture of aircraft, aircraft parts, and avionics equipment. They examine these materials to make sure they match the necessary design specifications. Inspectors may use hand tools and test instruments to accomplish this. They also issue the original certificates determining airworthiness for all aircraft. Inspectors in this area also inspect manufacturing facilities to make sure they meet safety regulations and standards.

Aviation safety inspectors working in airworthiness are concerned with the repair and maintenance of aircraft, aircraft parts, and avionics equipment. They assess the skills of the mechanics that work on aircraft and related parts and equipment and issue initial certification that they are proficient and meet the necessary requirements. This certification is done on a continuing basis, and the inspector is responsible for that as well. They are also responsible for assessing and certifying repair facilities and evaluating mechanic training programs. Inspectors perform inspections of aircraft to determine airworthiness, checking for any problems due to damage or deficient components. One way they do this is by starting the aircraft being inspected and observing the gauges, meters, and other instruments to ensure they are working properly. These inspectors are also responsible for examining maintenance programs and facilities, the equipment and procedures used for maintenance, and maintenance schedules. They advise whether new equipment needs to be acquired or if existing equipment needs to be fixed or modified. They check maintenance records and flight logs to see if prescribed service and maintenance procedures were performed and completed in a timely manner.

REQUIREMENTS

High School
High school students interested in a career in aviation safety should pursue a college preparatory curriculum, since a college degree is preferred for many positions in aviation safety inspection. Mathematics and science courses are especially useful. Course

work in communications will also be beneficial, since aviation safety inspectors need to ask questions, instruct others, and give oral and written reports of their findings.

Postsecondary Training
A high school diploma or equivalent is the minimum eligibility requirement for all federal aviation safety positions; a college degree may be required for nongovernment positions. Experience is also required, some of which is general to all aviation safety positions. Other experience is specific to the different positions in the field of aviation safety. A college education can be used to substitute for some or all of the required experience, depending upon each position. For example, the federal government will allow the substitution of one year of school for nine months of general experience. A bachelor's degree in the fields of engineering, aeronautics, or air transportation is especially useful. All prospective aviation safety inspectors should have general experience that provides them with knowledge of the aviation industry and/or aircraft operation. Examples of positions that would qualify as general experience include being a pilot or crew member, an air traffic controller, an aviation mechanic, or an avionics technician.

Some positions require specific experience. For example, an aviation safety inspector in operations needs experience as a pilot or copilot, a flight instructor, a flight test pilot, a flight inspector, or an aviation operations inspector. Some positions require that inspectors have the ability to operate specific types of aircraft. This experience can be gained from private flight schools, university flight schools, and military training.

An aviation safety inspector in manufacturing needs experience with quality control in accordance with federal aviation regulations. The quality control experience should be with the production of aircraft, aircraft engines, aircraft propellers, or aircraft assemblies. Some positions require additional experience in supervision, management, and implementation of quality control programs.

An aviation safety inspector focusing on airworthiness needs experience in supervising the repair and maintenance of aircraft, aircraft engines, or aircraft electronics communications and navigation systems. This experience must include being responsible for following federal aviation standards for airworthiness, or military regulations and safety standards. A job as a field service representative of an aircraft systems manufacturer or an aircraft equipment manufacturer may provide adequate experience for some positions, as well.

A Federal Aviation Administration aviation safety inspector *(right)*, the landowner *(center)*, and a firefighter view the wreckage of a small plane that crashed on private land in Amarillo, Texas. *(Michael Schumacher, AP Photo/Amarillo Globe-News)*

Certification or Licensing

Certification requirements vary according to the position. For example, an aviation safety inspector working for the federal government in a position where he or she has to operate aircraft must have a commercial pilot certificate as well as a flight instructor certificate, both with single and multiengine land and instrument ratings. An aviation safety inspector in a position where he or she has to operate aircraft in the air carrier field must have an airline transport pilot certificate. A commercial pilot certificate with multiengine land and instrument ratings, and eligibility for an airline transport pilot certificate will also suffice. Aviation safety inspectors in the area of manufacturing, working for the federal government at a GS-9 position or above, need an FAA mechanic certificate, with airframe and power plant ratings. All certificates must be current.

Other Requirements

Aviation safety inspectors must be methodical, have an eye for detail, and be able to accept responsibility. They must be persistent and patient as they perform inspections or follow an investigation to its conclusion. They also must be able to communicate well with others in order to reach a clear analysis of a situation and be able to report this information. Inspectors must be able to write effective reports that convey vast amounts of information and investigative work.

For many careers in aviation safety, U.S. citizenship is required, as well as the ability to pass a background security check. Some positions have a minimum age requirement.

EXPLORING

If you are interested in this career, you can begin exploring by arranging to shadow an aviation safety inspector at work. Talking with aviation safety inspectors and observing them as they work will give you a sampling of their duties, as well as the type of situations they encounter from day to day. Visits and interviews can be arranged through the FAA. Another option that will help you learn about the careers of aviation safety inspectors is to arrange to take a tour of an airport. Many aviation safety inspectors began with jobs such as aircraft pilots, air traffic controllers, and aviation mechanics or repair workers. Visiting an airport and taking a tour will give you a broader understanding of the basis of aviation safety and will enable you to observe how aviation safety issues affect those careers and the public travelers who pass in and out of an airport on a daily basis. Visits can be arranged through most airports and many airlines, although there might be limitations due to security concerns. You should be aware that every branch of the military services offers opportunities for vital experience for these jobs, and many jobs that are closely related.

EMPLOYERS

Most aviation safety inspectors are employed by the federal government, with the majority working for the Department of Transportation, namely the FAA, and the NTSB. Other employers of aviation safety inspectors include consulting firms, insurance companies, and companies that specialize in aviation technology and industry. Some inspectors are self-employed and work as independent consultants. Aviation safety inspectors are classified under the heading of transportation inspectors. There are approximately 26,000 transportation inspectors in the United States.

STARTING OUT

Aviation safety inspectors are generally not hired unless they have experience in the field of aviation, for example, as a pilot or crew member, an air traffic controller, an aviation mechanic, an avionics technician, or a manufacturing position in the aviation industry. A combination of work experience in the field of aviation and education in areas such as air transportation, engineering, or aeronautics will count as sufficient experience in some cases. After gaining the necessary experience, those interested in becoming an aviation safety inspector should apply for a position. One of the largest employers of aviation safety inspectors, the FAA, maintains a national register of qualified applicants. Persons interested in being hired by the FAA as an aviation safety inspector should contact the FAA for an application. Applicants who are deemed qualified and eligible for employment are placed on the national register for a period of one year. They are matched to any available job vacancies that fit their qualifications.

ADVANCEMENT

Aviation safety inspectors who demonstrate superior job skills may be promoted to positions with an increase in salary and greater responsibility. Those who exhibit managerial skills may advance to a supervisory position, such as section or branch chief. Inspectors with strong teaching and training skills may become instructors at the FAA Academy. Aviation safety inspectors who have a recognized level of expertise may opt to work for themselves as independent consultants.

EARNINGS

Transportation inspectors had median annual earnings of $55,250 in 2008, according to the U.S. Department of Labor. Salaries ranged from less than $27,560 to $101,010 or more annually. Inspectors who were employed in support activities for air transportation earned mean annual salaries of $50,190, while those employed in aerospace product and parts manufacturing earned $66,670.

Aviation safety inspectors receive typical fringe benefits, which may include medical and dental insurance, life insurance, sick days, paid vacation days, and participation in a 401(k) or similar savings plan. In addition, government employees may receive a pension. Self-employed aviation safety inspectors are responsible for their own insurance and savings needs.

WORK ENVIRONMENT

The work environment of an aviation safety inspector varies, depending on his or her employment situation. They usually work both indoors and outdoors, depending on the location and subject of the inspection or investigation. Many aviation safety inspectors who work for the government, consulting firms, or who are self-employed spend much time in the field and therefore will travel a great deal. Since they are responsible for inspecting aircraft and aircraft facilities, they will need to travel to the necessary locations in order to perform an inspection. Aviation safety inspectors investigating an accident will need to travel to the accident site. Aviation safety inspectors working for private companies may not need to travel as much, since many of their job duties will be performed in-house. Aviation safety inspectors need to be able to work independently and as part of a team, since both qualities are warranted in different job situations. A normal workweek for an aviation safety inspector is 40 hours. However, additional hours may be necessary, for example, to finish an important inspection or to investigate an accident.

OUTLOOK

The U.S. Department of Labor predicts that employment for transportation inspectors will grow faster than the average for all careers through 2018. Opportunities will also be very good for aviation safety inspectors as the federal government seeks to improve aviation safety and address security threats.

FOR MORE INFORMATION

For career information, contact
Federal Aviation Administration
800 Independence Avenue, SW
Washington, DC 20591-0001
Tel: 866-835-5322
http://www.faa.gov/careers

Avionics Engineers and Technicians

QUICK FACTS

School Subjects
Mathematics
Technical/shop

Personal Skills
Mechanical/manipulative
Technical/scientific

Work Environment
Primarily indoors
Primarily one location

Minimum Education Level
Bachelor's degree (engineers)
Some postsecondary training
(technicians)

Salary Range
$58,130 to $92,520 to
$134,570+ (engineers)
$34,220 to $49,310 to
$64,200+ (technicians)

Certification or Licensing
Required by all states (engineers)
Required for certain
positions (technicians)

Outlook
About as fast as the average
(engineers and technicians)

DOT
823

GOE
02.07.04. 02.08.04

NOC
2244

O*NET-SOC
17-2011.00, 17-3021.00,
49-2091.00

OVERVIEW

Avionics (from the words *aviation* and *electronics*) is the application of electronics to the operation of aircraft, spacecraft, and missiles. *Avionics engineers* conduct research and solve developmental problems associated with aviation, such as instrument landing systems and other safety instruments. Avionics engineers are a subspecialty of the field of aerospace engineering. There are approximately 71,600 aerospace engineers in the United States.

Avionics technicians inspect, test, adjust, and repair the electronic components of aircraft communications, navigation, and flight-control systems and compile complete maintenance-and-overhaul records for the work they do. Avionics technicians also calibrate and adjust the frequencies of communications apparatus when it is installed and perform periodic checks on those frequency settings. Avionics technicians hold about 18,800 jobs.

HISTORY

The field of avionics began in World War II, when military aircraft were operated for the first time using electronic equipment. Rockets were also being developed during this time, and these devices required electronic systems to control their flight. As aircraft rapidly grew more complicated, the amount of electronic apparatus needed for navigation and for monitoring equipment performance greatly increased. The World War II B-29 bomber carried 2,000 to 3,000 avionic components; the B-52 of the Vietnam era carried 50,000; later, the B-58 supersonic bomber required more than 95,000. As the military grew increasingly reliant on electronic systems, specialists were required to build, install, operate, and repair them.

The development of large ballistic missiles during and after World War II and the rapid growth of the U.S. space program after 1958 increased development of avionics technology. Large missiles and spacecraft require many more electronic components than even the largest and most sophisticated aircraft. Computerized guidance systems became especially important with the advent of manned spaceflights. Avionics technology was also applied to civil aircraft. The race to be the first in space and, later, to be the first to land on the moon stimulated the need for trained specialists to work with newer and more complex electronic technology. The push for achieving military superiority during the Cold War era also created a demand for avionics specialists and technicians. The commercial airline industry has been growing rapidly since the 1950s; since that time, more and more planes have been built, and the drive to provide greater comfort and safety for passengers has created an even greater demand for avionics engineers and technicians.

Avionics continues to be an important branch of aeronautical and astronautical engineering. The aerospace industry places great emphasis on research and development, assigning a much higher percentage of its trained technical personnel to this effort than is usual in industry. In addition, stringent safety regulations require constant surveillance of in-service equipment. For these reasons there is a high demand for trained and experienced avionics engineers and technicians to help in the development of new satellites, spacecraft, aircraft, and their component electronic systems and to maintain those in service.

THE JOB

Avionics engineers develop new electronic systems and components for aerospace use. Avionics technicians assist engineers in these developments. They also adapt existing systems and components for application in new equipment. For the most part, however, they install, test, repair, and maintain navigation, communications, and control apparatus in existing aircraft and spacecraft.

Technicians use apparatus such as circuit analyzers and oscilloscopes to test and replace such sophisticated equipment as transceivers and Doppler radar systems, as well as microphones, headsets, and other standard electronic communications apparatus. New equipment, once installed, must be tested and calibrated to prescribed specifications. Technicians also adjust the frequencies of radio sets and other communications equipment until the desired frequency has been achieved. Periodic maintenance checks and readjustments enable avionics technicians to keep equipment operating on proper frequencies. The technicians also complete and sign maintenance-and-overhaul documents recording the history of various equipment.

Avionics engineers and technicians involved in the design and testing of a new apparatus must take into account all operating conditions, determining weight limitations, resistance to physical shock, the atmospheric conditions the device will have to withstand, and other factors. For some sophisticated projects, technicians will have to design and make their tools first and then use them to construct and test new avionic components.

The range of equipment in the avionics field is so broad that technicians usually specialize in one area, such as radio equipment, radar, computerized guidance, or flight-control systems. New specialty areas are constantly opening up as innovations occur in avionics. The development of these new specialty areas requires technicians to keep informed by reading technical articles and books and by attending seminars and courses about the new developments, which are often sponsored by manufacturers.

Avionics technicians usually work as part of a team, especially if involved in research, testing, and development of new products. They are often required to keep notes and records of their work and to write detailed reports.

REQUIREMENTS

High School

Persons interested in pursuing a career in avionics should take high school mathematics courses at least through solid geometry and preferably through calculus. They should take English, speech, and communication classes in order to read complex and detailed technical articles, books, and reports; to write technical reports; and to present those reports to groups of people when required. Many schools offer shop classes in electronics and in diagram and blueprint reading.

Postsecondary Training

Avionics engineers must have a bachelor's degree from an accredited college or university and may participate in a cooperative education program through their engineering school. Avionics technicians must have completed a course of training at a postsecondary technical institute or community college. The training should include at least one year of electronics technician training. If not trained specifically in avionics, students should obtain a solid background in electronics theory and practice. Further specialized training will be done on the job, where technicians work with engineers and senior technicians until they are competent to work without direct supervision.

Larger corporations in the aerospace industry operate their own schools and training institutes. Such training rarely includes theoretical or general studies but concentrates on areas important to the company's functions. The U.S. Armed Forces also conduct excellent electronics and avionics training schools; their graduates are in high demand in the industry after they leave the service.

Certification or Licensing

All states require engineers to be licensed. There are two levels of licensing for engineers. Professional engineers (PEs) have graduated from an accredited engineering curriculum, have four years of engineering experience, and have passed a written exam. Engineering graduates need not wait until they have four years experience, however, to start the licensure process. Those who pass the Fundamentals of Engineering examination after graduating are called engineers in training (EITs) or engineer interns or intern engineers. The EIT certification usually is valid for 10 years. After acquiring suitable work experience, EITs can take the second examination, the Principles and Practice of Engineering exam, to gain full PE licensure.

In order to ensure that avionics engineers are kept up to date on their quickly changing field, many states have imposed continuing education requirements for relicensure.

Federal Communications Commission (FCC) regulations require that anyone who works with radio transmitting equipment have a restricted radiotelephone operator's license.

Avionics technicians must be certified by the FAA.

Other Requirements

To be successful in this work, you should have strong science and mathematics skills. In addition, you will need to have good manual dexterity and mechanical aptitude and the temperament for exacting work.

EXPLORING

One good way to learn more about avionics is to visit factories and test facilities where avionics technicians work as part of teams designing and testing new equipment. It is also possible to visit a large airfield's repair facilities where avionics technicians inspect, maintain, and calibrate communications and control apparatus. You can also arrange to visit other types of electronics manufacturers.

Useful information about avionics training programs and career opportunities is available from the U.S. Armed Forces as well as from trade and technical schools and community colleges that offer such programs. These organizations are always pleased to answer inquiries from prospective students or service personnel.

EMPLOYERS

About 49 percent of the 71,600 aerospace engineers employed in the United States work in the aerospace product and parts manufacturing industries. Other avionics engineers are employed in federal government agencies, primarily the Department of Defense and the National Aeronautics and Space Administration. Other employers include engineering and architectural services, research and testing services, and search and navigation equipment firms.

There are approximately 18,800 avionics technicians employed in the United States. Most technicians work for airlines or airports and flying fields. Other major employers include the federal government and aircraft assembly firms.

STARTING OUT

Those entering the field of avionics must first obtain the necessary training in electronics. Following that training, the school's career services department can help locate prospective employers, arrange interviews, and advise about an employment search. Other possibilities are to contact an employment agency or to approach a prospective employer directly. Service in the military is an excellent way to gain education, training, and experience in avionics; many companies are eager to hire technicians with a military background.

ADVANCEMENT

Avionics technicians usually begin their careers in trainee positions until they are thoroughly familiar with the requirements and routines of their work. Having completed their apprenticeships, they are usually assigned to work independently, with only minimal supervision, doing testing and repair work. The most experienced and able technicians go on to install new equipment and to work in research and development operations. Many senior technicians move into training, supervisory, sales, and customer relations positions. Some choose to pursue additional training and become avionics engineers.

Avionics engineers are already at an advanced position but may move up to become engineering supervisors or managers.

EARNINGS

The U.S. Department of Labor reports that median annual earnings of aerospace engineers (the category under which the department classifies avionics engineers) were $92,520 in 2008. Salaries ranged from less than $58,130 to more than $134,570. Median annual earnings of aerospace engineers who worked for the federal government were $103,810.

Median earnings of avionics technicians were $49,310 in 2008, according to the U.S. Department of Labor. The top paid 10 percent of technicians earned more than $64,200 a year. The lowest paid 10 percent earned less than $34,220 a year. Federal government employees (not including armed forces personnel) on the average earn slightly less than avionics technicians employed by private aerospace firms. Their jobs, however, are more secure.

Benefits for avionics engineers and technicians depend on the employer; however, they usually include such items as health insurance, retirement or 401(k) plans, and paid vacation days.

WORK ENVIRONMENT

Avionics engineers and technicians work for aircraft and aerospace manufacturers, airlines, and NASA and other government agencies. Most avionics engineers and technicians specialize in a specific area of avionics; they are also responsible for keeping up with the latest technological and industry advances. Their work is usually performed in pleasant indoor surroundings. Because this work is very precise, successful engineers and technicians must have a personality suited to meeting exact standards. Technicians sometimes work in closely cooperating teams. This requires an ability to work with a team spirit of coordinated effort.

OUTLOOK

The U.S. Department of Labor predicts that employment for both avionics engineers and technicians will grow about as fast as the average for all careers through 2018. Opportunities will be best for engineers and technicians who are employed in military and other government-related aerospace projects. Additionally, avionics technicians who are certified will have better employment prospects than those who do not have certification.

Avionics is an important and constantly developing field for which more and more trained engineers and technicians will be required. Reliance on electronic technology has grown rapidly and in virtually every industry. Many defense contractors have begun to branch out into other products, especially in the areas of electronic and computer technology. Commercial applications of the space program, including the launching of privately owned satellites, are also providing new opportunities in the aerospace industry.

The aerospace industry is closely tied to government spending and to political change, as well as to the economy, which also affects the aircraft and airline industries strongly. Opportunities will be best when the economy is strong and government and private-sector funding is available.

FOR MORE INFORMATION

For a list of accredited schools and colleges, contact
Accreditation Board for Engineering and Technology Inc.
111 Market Place, Suite 1050
Baltimore, MD 21202-7116
Tel: 410-347-7700
http://www.abet.org

Contact the association for publications with information on aerospace technologies, careers, and space.
Aerospace Industries Association
1000 Wilson Boulevard, Suite 1700
Arlington, VA 22209-3928
Tel: 703-358-1000
http://www.aia-aerospace.org

For career information and details on membership for high school students, contact
American Institute of Aeronautics and Astronautics
1801 Alexander Bell Drive, Suite 500
Reston, VA 20191-4344
Tel: 800-639-2422
http://www.aiaa.org

For information on educational programs and to purchase a copy of Engineering: Go For It, *contact*
American Society for Engineering Education
1818 N Street, NW, Suite 600
Washington, DC 20036-2479
Tel: 202-331-3500
http://www.asee.org

For information on general aviation, contact
General Aviation Manufacturers Association
1400 K Street, NW, Suite 801
Washington, DC 20005-2485
Tel: 202-393-1500
http://www.gama.aero/

For information on careers and student competitions, contact
Junior Engineering Technical Society
1420 King Street, Suite 405
Alexandria, VA 22314-2750
Tel: 703-548-5387
E-mail: info@jets.org
http://www.jets.org

For career and licensing information, contact
National Society of Professional Engineers
1420 King Street
Alexandria, VA 22314-2794
Tel: 703-684-2800
http://www.nspe.org/students

For information on careers in Canada, contact
Aerospace Industries Association of Canada
60 Queen Street, Suite 1200
Ottawa, ON K1P 5Y7 Canada
Tel: 613-232-4297
E-mail: info@aiac.ca
http://www.aiac.ca

Customs Officials

QUICK FACTS

School Subjects
English
Foreign language
Government

Personal Skills
Helping/teaching
Leadership/management

Work Environment
Indoors and outdoors
Primarily multiple locations

Minimum Education Level
Some postsecondary
training

Salary Range
$27,026 to $49,544 to
$59,383+

Certification or Licensing
None available

Outlook
About as fast as the average

DOT
168

GOE
04.03.01

NOC
1236

O*NET-SOC
33-3021.05

OVERVIEW

Customs officials are federal workers who are employed by the United States Bureau of Customs and Border Protection (a branch of the Department of Homeland Security) to prevent terrorists and terrorist weapons from entering the United States, enforce laws governing imports and exports, and to combat smuggling and revenue fraud. Amid a whirl of international travel and commercial activity, customs officials process travelers, baggage, cargo, and mail, as well as administer certain navigation laws. Stationed in the United States and overseas at airports, seaports, and all crossings, as well as at points along the Canadian and Mexican borders, customs officials examine, count, weigh, gauge, measure, and sample commercial and noncommercial cargoes entering and leaving the United States. It is their job to determine whether or not goods are admissible and, if so, how much tax, or duty, should be assessed on them. To prevent terrorism, smuggling, fraud, and cargo theft, customs officials also check the individual baggage declarations of international travelers and oversee the unloading of all types of commercial shipments. More than 57,500 customs workers are employed by Customs and Border Protection.

HISTORY

Countries collect taxes on imports and sometimes on exports as a means of producing revenue for the government. Export duties were first introduced in England in the year 1275 by a statute that levied

A U.S. Customs and Border Protection officer uses a highly sophisticated scanner to check for the presence of potentially dangerous material in travelers' luggage. *(James R. Tourtellotte, U.S. Customs and Border Protection)*

taxes on animal hides and on wool. American colonists in the 1700s objected to the import duties England forced them to pay (levied under the Townshend Acts), charging "taxation without representation." Although the British government rescinded the Townshend Acts, it retained the tax on tea, which led to the Boston Tea Party on December 16, 1773.

After the American Revolution, delegates at the Constitutional Convention decided that "no tax or duty shall be laid on articles exported from any state," but they approved taxing imports from abroad. The customs service was established by the First Congress in 1789 as part of the Treasury Department. Until 1816 these customs assessments were used primarily for revenue. The Tariff Act of 1816 declared, however, that the main function of customs laws was to protect American industry from foreign companies. By 1927 the customs service was established as a separate bureau within the Treasury Department.

Following the terrorist attacks of September 11, 2001, national attention was drawn to the need for heightened and new security at U.S. borders, in U.S. airports, and in dealing with travelers throughout the United States. Many governmental agencies, including the U.S. Customs Service, were restructured to better face this new threat. In 2003, the U.S. Customs Service was merged with portions of the Department of Agriculture, the Immigration and Naturalization Service, and the Border Patrol and renamed the Bureau of Customs and Border Protection (CBP). CBP became an official bureau of the Department of Homeland Security on March 1, 2003. According to its Web site, CBP's primary responsibility, in addition to controlling imports and exports, is to prevent international terrorist groups from securing weapons of mass destruction, arms and munitions, funds, and other support that could be used to commit acts of terrorism.

THE JOB

Customs officials perform a wide variety of duties, including preventing terrorists and terrorist weapons from entering the United States, controlling imports and exports, and combating smuggling and revenue fraud.

As a result of its merger in 2003 with several other protective and monitoring agencies of the U.S. government, the Bureau of Customs and Border Protection has created a new position, the *customs and border protection officer,* which consolidates the skills and responsibilities of three positions in these agencies: the customs inspector, the immigration officer, and the agricultural inspector. These workers are uniformed and armed. A second new position, the *CBP agriculture specialist* has been created to complement the work of the CBP officer. CBP Agriculture Specialists are uniformed, but not armed.

CBP officers conduct surveillance at points of entry into the United States to prohibit smuggling, detect customs violations, and deter acts of terrorism. They try to catch people illegally transporting smuggled merchandise and contraband such as narcotics, watches, jewelry, chemicals, and weapons, as well as fruits, plants, and meat that may be infested with pests or diseases. On the waterfront, officers monitor piers, ships, and crew members and are constantly on the lookout for items being thrown from the ship to small boats nearby. Customs patrol officers provide security at entrance and exit facilities of piers and airports, make sure all baggage is checked, and maintain security at loading, exit, and entrance areas of customs buildings and during the transfer of legal drug shipments to prevent hijackings or theft. Using informers and other sources, they gather intelligence information about illegal activities. When probable cause exists, they are authorized to take possible violators into custody, using physical force or weapons if necessary. They assist other customs personnel in developing or testing new enforcement techniques and equipment.

CBP officers also are responsible for carefully and thoroughly examining cargo to make sure that it matches the description on a ship's or aircraft's manifest. They inspect baggage and personal items worn or carried by travelers entering or leaving the United States by ship, plane, or automobile. CBP officers are authorized to go aboard a ship or plane to determine the exact nature of the cargo being transported. In the course of a single day they review cargo manifests, inspect cargo containers, and supervise unloading activities to prevent terrorism, smuggling, fraud, or cargo thefts. They may have to weigh and measure imports to see that commerce laws are being followed and to protect American distributors in cases where restricted trademarked merchandise is being brought into the country. In this way, they can protect the interests of American companies.

CBP officers examine crew and passenger lists, sometimes in cooperation with the police or security personnel from federal government agencies, who may be searching for criminals or terrorists. They are authorized to search suspicious individuals and to arrest these offenders if necessary. They are also allowed to conduct body searches of suspected individuals to check for contraband. They check health clearances and ships' documents in an effort to prevent the spread of disease that may require quarantine.

Individual baggage declarations of international travelers also come under their scrutiny. CBP officers who have baggage examination duty at points of entry into the United States classify purchases made abroad and, if necessary, assess and collect duties. All international travelers are allowed to bring home certain quantities of foreign purchases, such as perfume, clothing, tobacco, and liquor, without paying taxes. However, they must declare the amount and value of their purchases on a customs form. If they have made purchases above the duty-free limits, they must pay taxes. CBP officers are prepared to advise tourists about U.S. customs regulations and allow them to change their customs declarations if necessary and pay the duty before baggage inspection. CBP officers must be alert and observant to detect undeclared items. If any are discovered, it is up to the officer to decide whether an oversight or deliberate fraud has occurred. Sometimes the contraband is held and a hearing is scheduled to decide the case. A person who is caught trying to avoid paying duty is fined. When customs violations occur, officers must file detailed reports and often later appear as witnesses in court.

CBP agriculture specialists inspect agricultural and related goods that are imported into the United States. They act as agricultural experts at ports of entry to help protect people from agroterrorism and bioterrorism, as well as monitor agricultural imports for diseases and harmful pests.

CBP officers and CBP agriculture specialists cooperate with special agents from the Federal Bureau of Investigation, the Drug Enforcement Administration, the Food and Drug Administration, and other government agencies.

Some of the specialized fields in the Bureau of Customs and Border Protection are as follows.

Customs pilots, who must have a current Federal Aviation Administration (FAA) commercial pilot's license, conduct air surveillance of illegal traffic crossing U.S. borders by air, land, or sea. They apprehend, arrest, and search violators and prepare reports used to prosecute the criminals. They are stationed along the Canadian and Mexican borders as well as along coastal areas. They fly single- and multiengine planes and helicopters.

Canine enforcement officers train and use dogs to prevent smuggling of all controlled substances as defined by customs laws. These controlled substances include marijuana, narcotics, and dangerous drugs. After undergoing an intensive 15-week basic training course in the National Detector Dog Training Center, where each officer is paired with a dog and assigned to a post, canine enforcement officers work in cooperation with CBP officers to find and seize contraband and arrest smugglers. Canine enforcement officers also use dogs to detect bomb-making materials or other dangerous substances.

Import specialists become technical experts in a particular line of merchandise, such as wine or electronic equipment. They keep up to date on their area of specialization by going to trade shows and importers' places of business. Merchandise for delivery to commercial importers is examined, classified, and appraised by these specialists who must enforce import quotas and trademark laws. They use import quotas and current market values to determine the unit value of the merchandise in order to calculate the amount of money due the government in tariffs. Import specialists routinely question importers, check their lists, and make sure the merchandise matches the description and the list. If they find a violation, they call for a formal inquiry by customs special agents. Import specialists regularly deal with problems of fraud and violations of copyright and trademark laws. If the importer meets federal requirements, the import specialist issues a permit that authorizes the release of merchandise for delivery. If not, the goods might be seized and sold at public auction. These specialists encourage international trade by authorizing the lowest allowable duties on merchandise.

Customs and border protection chemists form a subgroup of import specialists who protect the health and safety of Americans. They analyze imported merchandise for textile fibers, lead content, narcotics, and presence of explosives or other harmful material. In many cases, the duty collected on imported products depends on the chemist's analysis and subsequent report. Customs chemists often serve as expert witnesses in court. Customs laboratories have specialized instruments that can analyze materials for their chemical components. These machines can determine such things as the amount of sucrose in a beverage, the fiber content of a textile product, the lead oxide content of fine crystal, or the presence of toxic chemicals and prohibited additives.

Criminal investigators, or *special agents,* are plainclothes investigators who make sure that the government obtains revenue on imports and that contraband and controlled substances do not enter or leave the country illegally. They investigate smuggling, criminal fraud, and major cargo thefts. Special agents target professional criminals as well as ordinary tourists who give false information on baggage declarations. Often working undercover, they cooperate with CBP officers and the FBI. Allowed special powers of entry, search, seizure, and arrest, special agents have the broadest powers of search of any law enforcement personnel in the United States. For instance, special agents do not need probable cause or a warrant to justify search or seizure near a border or port of entry. However, in the interior of the United States, probable cause but not a warrant is necessary to conduct a search.

REQUIREMENTS
High School
If you are interested in working for the U.S. Bureau of Customs and Border Protection, you should pursue a well-rounded education in high school. Courses in government, geography and social studies, English, and history will contribute to your understanding of international and domestic legal issues as well as give you a good general background. If you wish to become a specialist in scientific or investigative aspects of the CBP, courses in the sciences, particularly chemistry, will be necessary and courses in computer science will be helpful. Taking a foreign language, especially Spanish, will also help prepare you for this career.

Postsecondary Training
Applicants for CBP officer positions must be U.S. citizens and at least 21 years of age and no older than 36 years of age (although

On a Typical Day, the U.S. Customs and Border Protection Service . . .

Processes:

- Nearly 1.1 million passengers
- More than 70,450 truck, rail, and sea containers
- 331,347 vehicles

Executes:

- 73 arrests
- 614 refusals of entry at U.S. ports of entry
- 2,796 apprehensions at and in between ports of entry for illegal entry

Intercepts:

- 76 fraudulent documents
- One document for terrorism-related/national security concerns

Seizes:

- 7,621 pounds of narcotics
- 4,125 pounds of prohibited plant materials, meat, or animal products
- $295,829 in illicit or undeclared currency

Protects more than:

- 5,000 miles of border with Canada
- 1,900 miles of border with Mexico
- 95,000 miles of shoreline

Source: U.S. Bureau of Customs and Border Protection, 2008

those in law enforcement may be able to have this age limit waived). They must have earned at least a high school diploma, but applicants with college degrees are preferred. Applicants are required to have three years of general work experience involving contact with the public or four years of college.

Like all federal employees, applicants to CBP must pass a physical examination, undergo a security check, and pass a written test.

Entrance-level appointments are at grades GS-5 and GS-7, depending on the level of education or work experience.

New CBP officers participate in a rigorous 15-week training program at the Federal Law Enforcement Training Center near Brunswick, Georgia. Officers are trained in the following law enforcement skills: anti-terrorism; detection of contraband; interviewing; cross-cultural communications; firearms handling and qualification; immigration and naturalization laws; U.S. customs export and import laws, defensive tactics; arrest techniques; baton techniques; examination of cargo; bags and merchandise; border search exception; entry and control procedures; passenger processing; and officer safety and survival. Candidates who are chosen to work in locations that require fluency in Spanish may be required to undertake an additional six weeks of Spanish-language training. CBP agricultural specialists receive specialized training from the U.S. Department of Agriculture.

Other Requirements

Applicants must be in good physical condition, be emotionally and mentally stabile, and demonstrate the ability to correctly apply regulations or instructional material and make clear, concise oral or written reports. They must also be highly ethical and have excellent communication skills.

EXPLORING

There are several ways for you to learn about the various positions available at CBP. You can read *Frontline* (http://www.cbp.gov/xp/cgov/newsroom/publications/frontline_magazine), the official employee publication of the U.S. Bureau of Customs and Border Protection, to learn more about customs work. You can also talk with people employed as customs workers, consult your high school counselors, or contact local labor union organizations and offices for additional information. Information on federal government jobs is available from offices of the state employment service and area offices of the U.S. Office of Personnel Management.

Another great way to learn more about this career is to participate in the CBP Explorer Program. CBP Explorers receive practical and hands-on training in law enforcement and criminal justice fields. Applicants must be between the ages of 14 and 21 and have at least a C grade point average in high school or college. Participation in this program is also an excellent starting point for entry into the field. After one year in the program, Explorers can apply to the U.S. Customs Explorer Academy.

EMPLOYERS

The Bureau of Customs and Border Protection is the sole employer of customs workers. More than 57,500 people are employed by the agency.

STARTING OUT

Applicants may enter the various occupations of the Bureau of Customs and Border Protection by applying to take the appropriate civil service examinations. Interested applicants should note the age, citizenship, and experience requirements previously described and realize that they will undergo a background check and a drug test. If hired, applicants will receive exacting, on-the-job training.

ADVANCEMENT

All CBP workers have the opportunity to advance through a special system of promotion from within. Although they enter at the GS-5 or GS-7 level, after one year they may compete for promotion to supervisory positions or simply to positions at a higher grade level in the agency. The journeyman level is grade GS-11. Supervisory positions are available on a competitive basis.

EARNINGS

Entry-level positions at GS-5 began at a base annual pay of $27,026 in 2009, and those who started at the GS-7 level earned $33,477 per year. Most CBP officers are at the GS-11 position, which had a base annual salary of $49,544 in 2009. Supervisory positions beginning at GS-12 started at $59,383 in 2009. Federal employees in certain cities receive locality pay in addition to their salaries in order to offset the higher cost of living in those areas. Certain CBP workers are also entitled to receive Law Enforcement Availability Pay, which adds another 25 percent to their salaries. All federal workers receive annual cost-of-living salary increases. Federal workers enjoy generous benefits, including health and life insurance, pension plans, and holiday, sick leave, and vacation pay.

WORK ENVIRONMENT

The customs territory of the United States is divided into nine regions that include the 50 states, the District of Columbia, Puerto Rico, and the U.S. Virgin Islands. In these regions there are 327 ports of entry along land and sea borders. CBP workers may be assigned to any of these ports or to overseas work at airports, seaports, waterfronts, border stations, customs houses, or the U.S. Bureau of Customs and Border Protection headquarters in Washington, D.C. They are able to request assignments in certain localities and usually receive them when possible.

A typical work schedule is eight hours a day, five days a week, but CBP officers and related employees often work overtime or long into the night. U.S. entry and exit points must be supervised 24 hours a day, which means that workers rotate night shifts and weekend duty. CBP officers are sometimes assigned to one-person border points at remote locations, where they may perform immigration and agricultural inspections in addition to regular duties. They often risk physical injury from criminals violating customs regulations.

OUTLOOK

Employment at the Bureau of Customs and Border Protection is steady work that is not affected by changes in the economy. With the increased emphasis on law enforcement, especially the deterrence of terrorism, but also the detection of illegally imported drugs and pornography and the prevention of exports of sensitive high-technology items, the prospects for steady employment in the CBP are likely to grow and remain high. The U.S. Department of Labor predicts employment for police and detectives, a category including CBP officers, to grow about as fast as the average for all careers through 2018.

FOR MORE INFORMATION

For career information and to view a short video about CBP officers, visit the CBP Web site.
U.S. Customs and Border Protection
Department of Homeland Security
1300 Pennsylvania Avenue, NW
Washington, DC 20229-0002
Tel: 202-344-1130
http://www.cbp.gov/

Flight Attendants

OVERVIEW

Flight attendants are responsible for the safety and comfort of airline passengers from the initial boarding to disembarkment. They are trained to respond to emergencies and passenger illnesses. Flight attendants are required on almost all national and international commercial flights. There are approximately 98,700 flight attendants employed in the United States.

HISTORY

Although the first commercial passenger flights occurred as early as 1911, early airplane flights were not very comfortable. Airplanes were unstable, relatively small, and could not achieve very high altitudes. It was also difficult to operate passenger service at a profit. In the United States, the commercial aviation industry did not take off until the Kelly Air Mail Act of 1925, which encouraged the growth of the first commercial airlines. For many years, commercial airlines prospered because of profits from their airmail business. The government, in an effort to encourage passenger travel, offered airlines subsidies to lower the price of passenger tickets.

Concerns about the safety of airplanes kept many people from flying. In 1926, however, the Air Commerce Act, which established regulations and requirements for pilots and airlines and also defined an air-traffic system, improved consumer confidence in the airline industry. The famous flight of Charles Lindbergh the following year did much to promote public excitement about flying. Improvements such as stronger engines, better radio and navigational aids, and weather forecasting techniques were making flights safer. An important advancement in commercial air travel came with the development of the pressurized cabin. This meant that passengers could fly unaffected by the thin air of higher altitudes. As more people began to fly, the airlines sought ways to make flights even safer, more comfortable, and more enjoyable for the passenger. United Airlines was the first to offer special service to passengers in flight. In 1930, it hired graduate nurses to tend to passengers' comfort and needs. They were called stewardesses, after the similar position on cruise ships. Soon after, other airlines added stewardesses to their flights as well. At first, stewardesses performed many functions for the airlines, often acting as mechanics, refueling airplanes, loading passenger luggage and equipment necessary for the flight, as well as cleaning the interior of the airplane. But as airplanes grew larger and the numbers of passengers increased, these positions were filled by specialized personnel, and the stewardesses' responsibilities were devoted to the passengers. Stewardesses also began preparing and serving meals and drinks during flights.

The increasing growth and regulation of the airline industry brought still more duties for the flight attendant. Flight attendants began to instruct passengers on proper safety procedures, and they were required to make certain that safety factors were met before takeoff.

In the early years, most flight attendants were women, and the airlines often required that they remain unmarried in order to retain their jobs. Airlines also instituted age, height, and weight restrictions. Flight attendants were expected to provide a glamorous and pleasant image for airlines. During this time, employee turnover was very high. However, as the role of the flight attendant became more important and as regulations required them to perform more safety-oriented tasks, the image of the flight attendant changed as well. Because training flight attendants was expensive, the airlines began to offer better benefits and other incentives and removed some of their employee restrictions. Experience was also rewarded with higher pay, better benefits, and seniority privileges given according to the number of years worked. More and more flight attendants were making a career with the airlines. The introduction of Federal Aviation Administration (FAA) regulations requiring at least one flight attendant for every 50 passengers gave even greater growth and job security to this career.

Today, flight attendants fill more positions than any other airline occupation. The 98,700 flight attendants play a vital role in maintaining the safety and comfort in the skies. Many airlines are easing still more of their restrictions, such as age and weight limitations, as the role of the flight attendant has changed to require special training and skills.

THE JOB

Flight attendants perform a variety of pre-flight and in-flight duties. At least one hour before takeoff, they attend a briefing session with the rest of the flight crew; carefully check flight supplies, emergency life jackets, oxygen masks, and other passenger safety equipment; and see that the passenger cabins are neat, orderly, and furnished with pillows and blankets. They also check the plane galley to see that food and beverages to be served are on board and that the galley is secure for takeoff.

Attendants welcome the passengers on the flight and check their tickets as they board the plane. They show the passengers where to store briefcases and other small parcels, direct them to their cabin section for seating, and help them put their coats and carry-on luggage in overhead compartments. They often give special attention to elderly or disabled passengers and those traveling with small children.

Before takeoff, a flight attendant speaks to the passengers as a group, usually over a loudspeaker. He or she welcomes the passengers and gives the names of the crew and flight attendants, as well as weather, altitude, and safety information. As required by federal law, flight attendants demonstrate the use of lifesaving equipment and safety procedures and check to make sure all passenger seatbelts are fastened before takeoff.

Upon takeoff and landing and during any rough weather, flight attendants routinely check to make sure passengers are wearing their safety belts properly and have their seats in an upright position. They may distribute reading materials to passengers and answer any questions regarding flight schedules, weather, or the geographic terrain over which the plane is passing. Sometimes they call attention to points of interest that can be seen from the plane. They observe passengers during the flight to ensure their personal comfort and assist anyone who becomes airsick or nervous.

During some flights, attendants serve prepared breakfasts, lunches, dinners, or between-meal refreshments. They are responsible for certain clerical duties, such as filling out passenger reports and issuing reboarding passes. They keep the passenger cabins neat and comfortable during flights. Attendants serving on international flights may provide customs and airport information and sometimes translate flight information or passenger instructions into a foreign language. Most flight attendants work for commercial airlines. A small number, however, work on private airplanes owned and operated by corporations or private companies.

REQUIREMENTS

High School

Flight attendants need to have at least a high school education. A broad education is important to allow flight attendants to cope with the variety of situations they will encounter on the job. Beginning foreign language studies in high school will open up the possibility of working on international flights later.

Postsecondary Training

Because many airlines prefer to hire employees with some college experience, it is advisable to complete a two-year or four-year college degree. Although there is no specific major that will prepare you for a career as a flight attendant, degrees in psychology, public speaking, sociology, nursing, anthropology, hospitality, police or fire science, travel and tourism, and education are all good choices. A business degree with an emphasis in customer service or public relations is another excellent option. If you are especially interested in international flights, you might consider getting a degree in a foreign language.

Applicants with college-level education are often given preference in employment. Business training and experience working with the public are also assets. Attendants employed by international airlines are usually required to be able to converse in a foreign language.

Most large airline companies maintain their own training schools for flight attendants. Training programs may last from four to seven weeks. Some smaller airlines send their applicants to the schools run by the bigger airlines. A few colleges and schools offer flight attendant training, but these graduates may still be required to complete an airline's training program.

Airline training programs usually include classes in company operations and schedules, flight regulations and duties, first aid, grooming, emergency operations and evacuation procedures, flight terminology, and other types of job-related instruction. Flight attendants also receive 12 to 14 hours of additional emergency and passenger procedures training each year. Trainees for international flights are given instruction on customs and visa regulations and are taught procedures for terrorist attacks. Near the end of the training period, trainees are taken on practice flights, in which they perform their duties under supervision.

An on-the-job probationary period, usually six months, follows training school. During this time, experienced attendants pay close attention to the performance, aptitudes, and attitudes of the new attendants. After this period, new attendants serve as reserve personnel and fill in for attendants who are ill or on vacation. While on call, these reserve attendants must be available to work on short notice.

Certification or Licensing

All flight attendants must be certified by the Federal Aviation Administration (FAA). To become certified, flight attendants must complete training requirements (such as firefighting, medical emergency, evacuation, and security procedures) that have been created by the FAA and the Transportation Security Administration. They are certified for specific types of aircraft.

Other Requirements

Airlines in the United States require flight attendants to be U.S. citizens, have permanent resident status, or have valid work visas. In general, applicants must be at least 18 to 21 years old, although some airlines have higher minimum age requirements. They should be at least five feet, two inches tall in order to reach overhead compartments, and their weight should be in proportion to their height.

Airlines are particularly interested in employing people who are intelligent, poised, resourceful, and able to work in a tactful manner with the public. Flight attendants must have excellent health, good vision, and the ability to speak clearly. Young people who are interested in this occupation need to have a congenial temperament, a pleasant personality, and the desire to serve the public. They must be able to think clearly and logically, especially in emergency situations, and they must be able to follow instructions working as team members of flight crews.

EXPLORING

Opportunities for experience in this occupation are almost nonexistent until you have completed flight attendant training school. You may explore this occupation by talking with flight attendants or people in airline personnel offices. Airline companies and private training schools publish many brochures describing the work of flight attendants and send them out upon request.

Any part-time job in customer service, such as food service, hospitality, or retail sales, would be a good introduction to the kind of work flight attendants do. You might also try volunteering for jobs that require people skills, such as diplomacy, listening, helping, and explaining.

Read More About It

Bock, Becky S. *Welcome Aboard!: Your Career as a Flight Attendant.* 3d ed. Newcastle, Wash.: Aviation Supplies & Academics Inc., 2005.

Conway, Richard, and Paul Tizzard. *Flying Without Fear: 101 Fear of Flying Questions Answered.* London, U.K.: Flying Without Fear Publishing, 2008.

Marks, Marsha. *Flying by the Seat of My Pants: Flight Attendant Adventures on a Wing and a Prayer.* Colorado Springs, Colo.: WaterBrook Press, 2005.

Ward, Kiki. *The Essential Guide to Becoming a Flight Attendant.* Colleyville, Tex.: Kiwi Productions, 2008.

Whitelegg, Drew. *Working the Skies: The Fast-Paced, Disorienting World of the Flight Attendant.* New York: New York University Press, 2007.

EMPLOYERS

Approximately 98,700 professionally trained flight attendants are employed in the United States. Commercial airlines employ the vast majority of all flight attendants, most of whom are stationed in the major cities that serve as their airline's home base. A very small number of flight attendants work on company-owned or private planes.

STARTING OUT

Individuals who are interested in becoming flight attendants should apply directly to the personnel divisions of airline companies. The names and locations of these companies may be obtained by contacting the Air Transport Association of America. Addresses of airline personnel division offices can also be obtained from almost any airline office or ticket agency. Some major airlines have personnel recruiting teams that travel throughout the United States interviewing prospective flight attendants. Airline company offices can provide interested people with information regarding these recruitment visits, which are sometimes announced in newspaper advertisements in advance.

ADVANCEMENT

A number of advancement opportunities are open to flight attendants. They may advance to supervisory positions such as *first flight attendant* (sometimes known as the *flight purser* or the *supervising flight attendant*), or become an instructor or airline recruitment representative. They may also have the opportunity to move into the position of *chief attendant*, representing all flight attendants in a particular division or area. Although the rate of turnover in this field was once high, more people are making careers as flight attendants, and competition for available supervisory jobs is very high.

Many flight attendants who no longer qualify for flight duty because of health or other factors move into other jobs with the airlines. These jobs may include reservation agent, ticket agent, or personnel recruiter. They may also work in the public relations, sales, air transportation, dispatch, or communications divisions. Trained flight attendants may also find similar employment in other transportation or hospitality industries such as luxury cruise ship lines.

EARNINGS

Median annual earnings of flight attendants were $35,930 in 2008, according to the U.S. Department of Labor. The middle 50 percent earned between $28,420 and $49,910. Salaries ranged from less than $20,580 for the lowest paid 10 percent to more than $65,350 for the highest paid 10 percent.

Wage and work schedule requirements are established by union contract. Most flight attendants are members of the Association of Flight Attendants, the Transport Workers Union of America, or the International Brotherhood of Teamsters.

Flight attendants receive extra compensation for overtime and night flights. Flight attendants on international flights customarily earn higher salaries than those on domestic flights. Most airlines give periodic salary increases until a maximum pay ceiling is reached. Flight assignments are often based on seniority, with the most senior flight attendants having their choice of flight times and destinations.

Airlines usually pay flight attendants in training either living expenses or a training salary. Companies usually pay flight attendants' expenses such as food, ground transportation, and overnight accommodations while they are on duty or away from home base. Some airlines may require first-year flight attendants to purchase their own uniforms, but most companies supply them.

Fringe benefits include paid sick leave and vacation time, free or reduced air travel rates for attendants and their families, and, in some cases, group hospitalization and life insurance plans and retirement benefits.

WORK ENVIRONMENT

Flight attendants are usually assigned to a home base in a major city or large metropolitan area. These locations include New York, Chicago, Boston, Miami, Los Angeles, San Francisco, and St. Louis. Some airlines assign attendants on a rotation system to home bases, or they may give preference to the requests of those with rank and seniority on bids for certain home bases. Those with the longest records of service may be given the most desirable flights and schedules.

Flight attendants need to be flexible in their work schedules, mainly because commercial airlines maintain operations 24 hours a day throughout the entire year. They may be scheduled to work nights, weekends, and on holidays, and they may find that some of their allotted time off occurs away from home between flights. They are often away from home for several days at a time. Full-time flight attendants fly approximately 65–90 hours each month, and spend another 50 hours on the ground, preparing planes for flight, writing reports on completed flights, and waiting for planes that arrive late. Attendants work long days, but overall, they have more days off than employees in standard nine-to-five jobs.

The work performed by flight attendants may be physically demanding in some respects. For most of the flight, they are usually on their feet servicing passengers' needs, checking safety precautions, and, in many cases, serving meals and beverages. Working with the public all day can be draining. Flight attendants are the most visible employees of the airline, and they must be courteous to everyone, even passengers who are annoying or demanding. There is a certain degree of risk involved in any type of flight work. Flight attendants may suffer minor injuries as they perform their duties in a moving aircraft. They may suffer from irregular sleeping and eating patterns, dealing with stressful passengers, working in a pressurized environment, and breathing recycled air. Flight attendants also face risk of injury or death from hijackings. Since September 11, 2001, comprehensive security measures and upgrades have been implemented by airlines and the Transportation Security Administration to ensure the safety of travelers and industry workers.

The combination of free time and the opportunity to travel are benefits that many flight attendants enjoy. For those who enjoy helping and working with people, being a flight attendant may be a rewarding career.

OUTLOOK

The U.S. Department of Labor predicts that employment opportunities for flight attendants will grow about as fast as the average for all careers through 2018. The terrorist attacks of 2001 had a great impact on the airline industry, and several thousand flight attendants were subsequently laid off. The airline industry predicts a slow economic recovery as passengers only gradually return to the skies in pre-terrorist attack numbers. Economic and political conditions are likely to affect all airline employees over the next few years.

Even in the best of times, finding employment as a flight attendant is highly competitive, and since some job restrictions at airlines have been abolished, the once high rate of turnover for flight attendants has declined. Even though the number of job openings is expected to grow, airlines receive thousands of applications each year. Most of the job openings through 2018 will arise from replacement of flight attendants who retire or transfer to other jobs. Students interested in this career will have a competitive advantage if they have a college degree and prior work experience in customer relations or public contact. Courses in business, psychology, sociology, geography, speech, communications, first aid and emergency medical techniques such as CPR, and knowledge of foreign languages and cultures will make the prospective flight attendant more attractive to the airlines.

Job opportunities may be strongest at regional and commuter, low-cost, and charter airlines, as well as with companies that have private jets for their executives.

FOR MORE INFORMATION

For industry and statistical information, as well as to read The Airline Handbook *online, visit the association's Web site.*
Air Transport Association of America
1301 Pennsylvania Avenue, NW, Suite 1100
Washington, DC 20004-1738
Tel: 202-626-4000
E-mail: ata@airlines.org
http://www.airlines.org

For information on union membership, contact
Association of Flight Attendants-CWA
501 Third Street, NW
Washington, DC 20001-2760

Tel: 202-434-1300
E-mail: info@afacwa.org
http://www.afanet.org

This union represents more than 18,000 flight attendants who are employed by American Airlines.
Association of Professional Flight Attendants
1004 West Euless Boulevard
Euless, TX 76040-5009
Tel: 800-395-2732
http://www.apfa.org

For information on aviation safety, statistics, and regulations, contact
Federal Aviation Administration
800 Independence Avenue, SW
Washington, DC 20591-0001
Tel: 866-835-5322
http://www.faa.gov

This Web site offers information on careers and job issues and links to discussion forums and other aviation-related sites.
Flight Attendants.org
http://www.flightattendants.org

Flight Instructors

QUICK FACTS

School Subjects
Mathematics
Physics

Personal Skills
Leadership/management
Technical/scientific

Work Environment
Indoors and outdoors
Primarily multiple locations

Minimum Education Level
Some postsecondary training

Salary Range
$12,300 to $40,530 to
$75,000+

Certification or Licensing
Required by all states

Outlook
About as fast as the average

DOT
097, 099, 196

GOE
07.03.01

NOC
2271

O*NET-SOC
25-1194.00, 53-2011.00,
53-2012.00

OVERVIEW

Flight instructors are pilots who use their experience, knowledge, joy of flying, and ability to explain complex subjects to teach students how to fly aircraft. Flight instructors give classroom as well as hands-on flying instruction to their students. Topics covered include aerodynamics, navigation, instrument reading, aircraft control techniques, and federal aviation regulations. They may teach at flight schools, for airlines, in the military, or work as self-employed instructors. There are approximately 109,000 flight instructors working in the United States.

HISTORY

People have been interested in figuring out how to fly for hundreds of years. Before the 20th century, however, attempts at flying were generally based on self-taught methods and self-experimentation. Flying enthusiasts generally studied the efforts of others and created their own aircraft (or what they hoped would be aircraft). In 1903, Orville and Wilbur Wright completed their first flight with a powered flying machine and began the period of modern aviation. In 1906, Alberto Santos-Dumont completed the first flight in Europe, and in 1909 Louis Blériot made the first flight across the English Channel, flying from France to England in slightly more than 30 minutes.

By the 1920s the commercial benefits of airplanes—flying mail, goods, and people—had become apparent and more and more people were interested in using flight and learning to fly. The federal government became involved in regulating the aviation field with the passing of the Air Commerce Act in 1926. With this act, the Department of Commerce took responsibility for such actions as issuing and enforcing air traffic rules, setting standards for pilot certification (licensing), and establishing airways. A significant development in teaching methods occurred a few years later, when in 1929 Edwin Link invented the Link trainer. The Link trainer, a flight simulator, was a ground-operated machine that simulated flying conditions and reduced some of the time, expense, and danger of training new pilots. Advances in flight were spurred by both World War I and World War II, when the military use of aircraft became a major focus of the aviation industry. The military also provided an environment for training pilots, and other crew members, in an organized and uniform process.

In the meantime, government oversight of the field continued to grow, and in 1938 the regulation of aviation was transferred from the Department of Commerce to a new agency—the Civil Aeronautics Authority. This organization eventually grew into what is now the Federal Aviation Administration (FAA). The FAA is responsible for setting and enforcing rules of air safety, traffic, and education. The days of trying to figure out how to fly on one's own are gone; today's pilots must complete extensive training and education before the FAA grants flight instructor certification.

THE JOB

Simply put, the job of a flight instructor combines both the work of a pilot and the work of a teacher. In order to teach others how to fly, flight instructors must first become pilots themselves, learning how to command an aircraft in flight as well as taking care of responsibilities on the ground. Although flight instructors fly with students, it is the instructor who is ultimately responsible for making sure all appropriate pre-flight, in-flight, and afterlanding procedures are followed. Therefore, like any pilot, instructors must know how to complete such pre-flight duties as making sure the aircraft is properly maintained and has the right amount of fuel, preparing a flight plan and knowing the latest weather conditions, and testing the airplane's instruments and controls. In flight, the instructor's piloting duties include monitoring the airplane's systems, paying attention to weather conditions, and making sure there is communication with air traffic control. Some of the afterlanding duties instructors must know how to complete are shutting down the airplane, explaining any problems to the maintenance crew, and updating their flight logbooks.

In addition to all the skill, knowledge, and experience needed to complete these and other pilot tasks, instructors have teaching responsibilities. Flight instructors may work on their own, offering private lessons, or at ground schools that are at an airport, part of a major airline, in the military, or at a university. Their teaching duties include deciding what classes to offer, making a syllabus, scheduling class times, and picking out the textbooks and other materials that the students will need. Instructors must know current federal aviation regulations so that they can teach correct rules to their students. Flight instructors should also be up to date on the latest teaching technologies available. Computer-based programs and flight simulators, for example, are often used in flight instruction, and instructors should be able to make use of these resources.

Flight instructors, like other kinds of teachers, spend time outside of the classroom preparing for what they will teach. They may write lectures, make PowerPoint presentations, arrange for demonstrations of equipment, and grade tests or otherwise keep track of each student's progress. Subjects that instructors cover during class meetings include principles of aerodynamics, the national airspace system, navigation, meteorology, instrument reading, and proper use of radio communications. They also demonstrate how to use equipment and discuss the functions of parts of an airplane, such as rudders, flaps, and elevators. Another important classroom activity is overseeing students' use of flight simulators. A flight simulator is made to look and feel like the cockpit of an airplane, with instrument panels and a pilot's seat. In the simulator students can practice maneuvers such as taking off, flying, and landing. Instructors are able to monitor a student's actions while in the simulator, and they can use a control panel to change conditions during the student's simulated flight. This helps students develop skills they will need when faced with changing conditions in real-life flying situations. After a session in the flight simulator, the instructor and student review the student's actions and discuss what was done well, what needs improvement, and how to work on these areas.

Taking students on training flights is another important part of a flight instructor's work. Aircraft that are designed for training have two sets of controls and a cockpit arranged so that the student and instructor sit either side by side or one in front of the other. Because there are two sets of controls, the instructor can observe the student's flying but also be able to take back control of the plane if the student needs help. During training flights, instructors can show students how to handle the plane in different situations, how to use instruments like the altimeter and vertical speed indicator, and how to do maneuvers that may help the student during a dangerous situation in the future. Safety is a top priority for instructors and they may take students through emergency situations, such as a stall, to teach them how to react. Flight instructors also teach students how to maintain a flight logbook. Each student must record information about the flights he or she makes, such as what was done on the flight, how long the flight took, and the flight's distance. In addition, instructors need to keep their own "teacher's logbook" with information on each student. These logbooks must be kept by instructors for at least three years after they have had a student.

Before flight instructors can let students make their first solo flight, the students must get a medical certificate (certifying they are in good health) and an instructor-endorsed student pilot certificate. In order to get the student pilot certificate, the student must pass a test given by the flight instructor. This test will have questions about FAA rules as well as questions about the model and make of the aircraft the student will fly. If the student passes the test and the instructor feels the student is prepared to make a solo flight, the instructor will sign—or endorse—the student pilot certificate and the student logbook. The flight instructor's work isn't done yet, though; they continue to work with students until the students complete all their training and get their FAA pilot's certificate (sometimes called a license).

Not all students are beginners. Some students are already pilots who want to become certified as another type of pilot or for another type of aircraft. Someone with a recreational pilot's certificate, for example, may want to get a private pilot's certificate. Someone with a private pilot's certificate may want to get a commercial pilot's certificate. Someone else may want to earn a certificate for flying multiengine planes. Flight instructors are only allowed to teach the categories for which they are already certified. Because of this, instructors are often students themselves, spending their spare time learning how to operate different aircraft and getting various certifications. Many instructors see this need to expand on their flying skills and certifications as an opportunity for both professional achievement and personal satisfaction.

REQUIREMENTS

High School

Remember that if you want to work as a flight instructor, you'll have to become a pilot first. So take classes in high school that will prepare you for college. Chemistry, physics, algebra, geometry, and other advanced science and math classes are important to take. Since a career in this field demands extensive use of technology, be sure to take computer courses. To help you develop your teaching skills, take English or communication classes—these will improve your writing and speaking abilities. You may also want to take acting or drama classes as well as psychology. Again, these classes should help you with teaching skills such as commanding an audience and learning to understand others.

Postsecondary Training

Although the FAA does not require flight instructors to have a particular degree, a college education is highly recommended. You may want to attend a university with a specialized aviation program. If you prefer, though, you can take a broader course of study at any college. Continue your math and science studies, taking courses such as aerodynamics, physics, and college algebra. Classes in geography and meteorology are also helpful. If your school offers classes in the fundamentals of teaching or instruction, take these as well. And, naturally, keep up with your computer skills. Another option is to get your pilot training in the military, and you may want to contact your local recruiting offices for more information.

If you do not attend a specialized aviation program or get your training in the military, you will need to get flight instruction, either from an instructor who offers private lessons or through a flight school, also known as pilot school. The FAA provides information on pilot schools; visit http://www.faa.gov to find out more. As you learn how to fly, be aware of your school experience as well. What does your instructor do that you like or find helpful? Do you like the size of the school and the equipment there? After all, answers to questions like these may help you determine where you want to work eventually as an instructor.

Certification or Licensing

To become a flight instructor, you will need to get FAA flight-instructor certification. To do this, you must have a commercial pilot's certification for the kind of aircraft (single engine, multi-engine, instrument, and so on) that matches the flight instructor rating (designation) you want to have. You must have accumulated a certain amount of flying time and have your logbook properly endorsed. You must have completed training that covered topics such as evaluation of student flight performance, lesson planning, and how to properly instruct on stall awareness, spin entry, spins, and spin-recovery methods. In addition, you will need to pass a test with written and oral sections as well as a flight test.

Types of Pilot Licenses

Student pilot certificate (license): Used for the initial training period of flying. Student pilots must fly with a flight instructor and can only fly solo after receiving appropriate endorsements from their flight instructor.

Recreational pilot certificate: Limits the pilot to specific classes and categories of aircraft, a limited number of passengers, the distance that may be flown from the point of departure, and flight into controlled airports.

Private pilot certificate: Allows a pilot to carry passengers and use his or her aircraft for limited business purposes.

Commercial pilot certificate: Allows a pilot to fly for compensation and hire.

Airline transport pilot certificate: Required to fly as captain by some air transport operations.

Source: Federal Aviation Administration

The National Association of Flight Instructors offers several professional certifications, including the associate master flight instructor, the master flight instructor, and the master ground instructor designations. These certifications are voluntary and demonstrate commitment to the profession. To earn these, an instructor must meet certain requirements, such as being a member of the association, having FAA flight instructor certification, and completing a certain amount of continuing education credits or activities.

Other Requirements

You must pass a physical exam and be certified fit to fly. Naturally, anyone controlling an aircraft needs to have good vision. So you must have eyesight of 20/20 or better in each eye, although you can wear glasses or contact lenses to get this. Good hearing is also a requirement. In addition to physical and intellectual requirements, flight instructors need to be calm, have good judgment, be able to deal well with people, and, of course, have a love of flying.

EXPLORING

You can explore aspects of this field while you are still in high school. Begin by reading aviation magazines as well as more complex materials with FAA rules and other information. The FAA publishes study materials covering topics such as aviation weather, aeronautical knowledge, and weight and balance. Its Web site has information on how to get these study guides. You can also begin developing radio skills, which you will need as a pilot, by learning to use a ham radio.

Although you must be at least 16 to get a student pilot certificate for solo flying, you can start taking flying lessons even if you're younger. This will allow you to see how much you enjoy the flying experience as well as let you work with a flight instructor and, in that way, get a close-up view of the instructor's job. If you can't afford lessons, you can still meet and interview a local flight instructor to get information about this type of work.

Another fun thing to do is to go to air shows, which are frequently held during the summers. Check for shows or "fly-ins" in your area or plan a trip to one. The Experimental Aircraft Association (EAA) holds one of the largest such fly-ins each summer in Oshkosh, Wisconsin, as well as other regional fly-ins across the country. At these shows you can meet other flying enthusiasts, see every kind of aircraft from homebuilts (those built by the pilots themselves) to sophisticated military aircraft, attend workshops, and watch flying demonstrations. The EAA also offers Air Academy Aviation Camps for those ages 12 to 18 as well as weekend "camps" for adults and a free Young Eagles Flight Program that matches young people between the ages of eight and 17 who are fascinated by flight with adult pilots eager to share their enthusiasm for aviation. Young Eagles actually fly with the pilots, and flights last 15–20 minutes. Membership is also available. For more information about these opportunities, visit http://www.eaa.org.

EMPLOYERS

Flight instructors who are in the military are employed by the U.S. government. In the civilian world, flight instructors are typically employed by flight schools or they may work independently, offering lessons on their own. Some instructors may begin by working at an established flight school but have the goal of eventually running their own school. Flight schools are located all across the country, and many airports have them. The warmer months of the year tend to be busiest for flight instructors because this is when it is easiest to take beginners out for training flights. Of course, flight instructors working in locations where the weather is fairly warm all year usually do not experience such fluctuations. Schools are classified as FAA-approved or nonapproved. This is based on factors such as the amount and type of equipment, personnel, and facilities the school has. Many nonapproved schools offer excellent training but do not seek FAA approval simply because of their smaller size or other factors. Approximately 109,000 flight instructors are employed in the United States, but because some flight instructors combine this work with other work, such as piloting chartered flights, it is difficult to determine the exact number of these workers.

STARTING OUT

Since pilots need to log flying time as one requirement for gaining different certifications, a number of people choose to begin their careers as flight instructors. Then as they gain time and experience they may move on to other positions, such as pilot at a major airline, which is their ultimate goal. Some flight instructors start out as military pilots and then become instructors later in their professional lives. Another way to gain entry into the field is through connections made at flight school. In fact, some students who have impressed their instructors may be offered a job there.

ADVANCEMENT

Advancement often depends on the individual's goals. Some instructors may want to advance to the point of running their own schools. An instructor working at a small airport school may want to move on to work at a large school in a metropolitan area or at a school that is part of a university. And other instructors may simply want to increase the number of students they teach. No matter what the goal, however, the best way to make any type of advancement in this field is by gaining as much personal flying experience as possible and becoming certified to pilot a variety of aircraft. It is extremely important for those in this career to keep up with new technologies, regulations, and other developments. Only those who are willing to continuously challenge themselves to increase their skills and knowledge will advance the most.

EARNINGS

Flight instructors' earnings vary based on factors such as the size and type of employer, the type of aircraft used, and the amount of experience the instructor has. According to the FAA, instructors working at flight schools may earn from $12,300 to $40,530 a year. A few flight instructors with extensive experience and working for major airlines may earn as much as $75,000 or more a year. Instructors who work independently (that is, are self-employed) typically charge an hourly fee, which may be approximately between $30 and $50 an hour. Their yearly income, though, depends on the number of students they have and the amount of time they are actually able to spend teaching.

The benefits a flight instructor receives depend on the employer. For example, those working at colleges or universities typically receive the same health insurance, paid vacation time, and retirement plans as other teachers there. At major airlines, instructors also typically get health insurance, paid vacation and sick time, and retirement plans. In addition, they may get stock options through the company. Those working at small, nonapproved schools may get a minimum of health insurance and little or no retirement plan. And instructors who are self-employed do not receive any benefits.

WORK ENVIRONMENT

Flight instructors work in classrooms and in aircraft, and they must be comfortable working with computers, machines, and people. In order to accommodate their students' schedules, many instructors hold classes in the evenings or on weekends. FAA rules limit the number of hours per day that a flight instructor can spend giving in-flight instruction; however, instructors can spend as much time as they want doing classroom work. On average, instructors work between 40 and 50 hours a week. Those who work at small schools or independently may spend part of their time teaching and part of their time doing other flying jobs to supplement their income.

Instructors must be able to deal with stressful situations in the air, including mechanical problems, sudden changes in weather, and students' fears or mistakes.

OUTLOOK

The U.S. Department of Labor estimates that employment for all types of pilots will grow at an average rate through 2018. However, the department also notes that the growth rate depends a great deal on both the pilot's specific occupation and the overall condition of the economy. When the economy is bad, fewer people will be able to afford such expenses as flying lessons. With a decrease in student enrollment, flight schools will hire fewer instructors. Additionally, instructors who are working will be more likely to keep those jobs than to move into other positions, such as airline pilot, and make way for new flight instructors.

FOR MORE INFORMATION

For information on its aviation camps, contact
EAA Air Academy
3000 Poberezny Road
Oshkosh, WI 54902-8939
Tel: 888-322-3229
E-mail: airacademy@eaa.org
http://www.eaa.org/airacademy

For information about fly-ins, various aircraft, and membership, contact
Experimental Aircraft Association
EAA Aviation Center
3000 Poberezny Road
Oshkosh, WI 54902-8939
Tel: 920-426-4800
http://www.eaa.org

For more information about the history of the FAA, pilot schools, and certification, contact
Federal Aviation Administration (FAA)
800 Independence Avenue, SW
Washington, DC 20591-0001
Tel: 866-835-5322
http://www.faa.gov

For information on professional certifications, contact
National Association of Flight Instructors
c/o EAA Aviation Center
PO Box 3086
Oshkosh, WI 54903-3086
Tel: 920-426-6801
E-mail: nafi@eaa.org
http://www.nafinet.org

Ground Services Workers

QUICK FACTS

School Subjects
Mathematics
Physical education
Technical/shop

Personal Skills
Following instructions
Mechanical/manipulative

Work Environment
Indoors and outdoors
Primarily multiple locations

Minimum Education Level
High school diploma

Salary Range
$12,480 to $20,800 to
$37,440

Certification or Licensing
Required for certain positions

Outlook
More slowly than the average

DOT
248, 352, 357, 919

GOE
11.01.01, 11.03.01, 11.05.01

NOC
6661, 7437

O*NET-SOC
35-1011.00, 39-6011.00,
43-5011.00, 53-1011.00,
53-2022.00, 53-7062.03

OVERVIEW

Ground services workers play a significant role in the aviation process. They ensure the safety, security, and comfort of passengers, oversee the loading and unloading of cargo and baggage, and prepare aircraft for flight. Their level of organization determines how smoothly the flight process will be for passengers and flight crew.

HISTORY

For as long as aircraft have been taking off and landing at airports, there has been a need for ground services workers. But it wasn't until after World War II that the commercial airline industry began to grow and prosper. New airlines emerged to compete for the business of air travelers, and many ground services workers were needed to maintain aircraft, process and transport baggage and cargo, prepare food for flights, refuel planes, and perform countless other tasks. Today, ground services workers play an integral role in the success and efficient functioning of our nation's 517 commercial service airports.

THE JOB

There are many different types of ground services workers. *Air freight agents* oversee the shipment of air freight. They receive shipments and supervise the loading and unloading of freight. *Ramp service workers* are responsible for keeping the exterior of the aircraft in top shape. They wash and polish the plane, touch up paint, and perform other necessary cleaning tasks.

Linepersons meet the arriving aircraft and guide it to an appropriate parking area. They secure the aircraft, check for fluid leaks or changes in tire pressure, and often serve as a greeter to passengers. At smaller facilities, linepersons may also coordinate rental cars, catering, and other services for passengers and employees.

Between flights, *ramp agents* prepare for arriving aircraft by readying the wheellocks, beltloaders (for baggage unloading), and other machinery used for landing and takeoff. Ramp agents also perform maintenance tasks such as spraying de-icing solution on the plane's wings during winter conditions and keeping the landing area free of debris.

Drivers transport supplies, equipment, and people throughout the airport. They include drivers of food trucks, mobile stairs, cleaning equipment, aviation fuel, and other supplies. These workers also drive maintenance specialists and other employees to specified terminals and aircraft in a timely manner.

Cabin service workers clean the inside of the airplane and the cockpit in between flights. These workers, who are also referred to as *aircraft servicers*, replace headrests, fold blankets, and fill seat backs with magazines and safety information. Cabin service workers vacuum, pick up trash, wash windows and bathrooms, and ensure the overall cleanliness of the interior of the plane.

Baggage and air cargo handlers load and unload baggage, airmail, and air express and air cargo shipments for passengers. They must be both careful and precise in the handling and placement of baggage. Handlers must sort and stack baggage in the underside of the airplane, positioning luggage so that different groups of passengers will have access to their luggage at different destinations. Baggage handling involves heavy lifting and is a physically demanding occupation. There is little room for error as a baggage and air cargo handler. *Baggage service agents* assist passengers with delayed, lost, or damaged luggage.

Aircraft fuelers, along with drivers, operate fueling equipment. *Fuel truck drivers* transport the aviation fuel to the waiting aircraft, and the fueler then climbs onto the wings of the plane with a hose and fills it with fuel. Workers in this occupation need to be agile and able to work under deadline pressure.

Food service workers prepare meals that are served during flights. They follow set recipes to prepare the food, and they make sure they have the correct number of serving dishes for each flight. Food service workers place the food in containers for pickup and also clean dirty dishes. Other food service workers are employed in airport restaurants and bars.

A baggage handler hoists a piece of luggage off the ramp and onto a waiting trailer as he helps unload an airplane at Denver International Airport. (*David Zalubowski, AP Photo*)

Operations agents ensure that the flight process runs smoothly for both passengers and employees. They keep track of the number of passengers and pieces of luggage. Operations agents communicate information to and from pilots, ground crews, and aircraft fuelers. If a flight is overbooked, operations agents must make decisions to remedy the situation and keep passengers calm.

All ground service workers must be efficient, precise, and timely in their work. Their preparation and attention to detail makes the flight process enjoyable and safe for those aboard the aircraft.

REQUIREMENTS

High School

High school courses that will help prepare you for this career include computer science, mathematics, and shop. Since many of these positions require workers to lift or move heavy loads, taking physical education classes and participating in sports will help you build your physical strength and endurance. If you are interested in the career of air freight agent or operations agent, be sure to take as many business, mathematics, accounting, and computer classes as possible. If your interests lie more in the area of food preparation, classes in family and consumer science and health will help you prepare for work in these careers.

Postsecondary Training

Although most ground services jobs are entry level and require only a high school diploma (or the equivalent), many airlines like job applicants to have some general postsecondary education.

Certification or Licensing

In most states, airport and other professional drivers must qualify for a commercial driver's license. State motor vehicle departments can provide information on how to qualify for this license. Food service workers are required by law in most states to possess a health certificate and to be examined periodically. These examinations, usually given by the state board of health, make certain that the individual is free from communicable diseases and skin infections. Aircraft fuelers must meet rules and regulations established by the Federal Aviation Administration (FAA). They often satisfy these requirements through employer-administered certification.

Other Requirements

All ground services workers should have good communication and teamwork skills and be able to work quickly. Workers who drive vehicles and ground equipment need to have a valid driver's license. Baggage handlers and ramp agents must be able to lift heavy baggage, cargo, or equipment, as well as operate machinery. Baggage service agents must have excellent people skills in order to deal with passengers who are angry or frustrated by lost or damaged luggage. Fuelers should have a basic aptitude for machinery and equipment. Age requirements for these positions vary by employer, but most require applicants to be at least 18 to 21 years of age.

EXPLORING

One of the best ways to learn about a career in ground services is to talk with a worker in the field. Ask your teacher or guidance counselor to set up an information interview with an aircraft servicer, baggage and cargo handler, or other worker in the field.

EMPLOYERS

Airlines, airports, and airport service contractors are the primary employers of ground services workers.

STARTING OUT

Employment as a ground services worker is an excellent way to break into the aviation industry. Contact airlines, airports, and airport service contractors directly for possible job leads. These positions are also often listed in the classified sections of newspapers.

ADVANCEMENT

With hard work, dedication, and additional education or training, ground services workers can advance to a variety of managerial and supervisory positions. For example, air freight agents can advance to the position of supervisor of air freight handlers or ramp service planner. Food service workers can become chefs or food service managers. Cabin service workers can advance to positions as drivers, aircraft fuelers, and baggage and cargo handlers. A very experienced worker who earns a college degree in airport management, business administration, or engineering can become an assistant airport manager or airport manager.

EARNINGS

Salaries for ground services workers vary based on the size and location of the airport and the worker's job description and level of experience. Entry-level workers may initially earn minimum wage. The Federal Aviation Administration reports the following annual salary ranges by profession: air freight agents, $15,000 to $31,000; ramp service workers and linepersons, $14,560 to $31,200; ramp agents, $13,520 to $15,600; aircraft servicers, $12,480 to $14,560; baggage and cargo handlers, $12,480 to $37,440; aircraft fuelers, $16,640 to $20,800; food service workers, $12,480 to $18,720; and operations agents and drivers, $14,560 to $16,640.

Ground services workers receive typical fringe benefits, including medical and dental insurance, life insurance, paid sick and vacation days, and the opportunity to participate in a 401(k) or similar savings plan.

WORK ENVIRONMENT

Ground services areas are typically noisy, hectic, and sometimes dangerous settings as workers go about their duties, luggage and cargo are loaded and unloaded, and heavy equipment and conveyor belts are used to ready an aircraft for flight. Ground services employees often work outdoors in all types of weather. Most ground services workers are required to wear uniforms for security purposes, as well as earplugs and other protective equipment to ensure their safety. Since flights arrive and depart 24 hours a day, seven days a week, ground services workers may be required to work nights and weekends.

OUTLOOK

Employment in the air transportation industry is expected to grow more slowly than the average through 2018, according to the U.S. Department of Labor (DOL). Commercial air travel has decreased as a result of the weak economy, creating less need for airport workers. Passenger and cargo traffic is expected to rebound slowly over the next several years. The DOL predicts that employment opportunities will be good for ground services workers, such as baggage handlers and aircraft cleaners, as a result of high turnover in these occupations.

FOR MORE INFORMATION

To read The Airline Handbook, *visit the ATAA Web site.*
Air Transport Association of America (ATAA)
1301 Pennsylvania Avenue, NW, Suite 1100
Washington, DC 20004-1738
Tel: 202-626-4000
E-mail: ata@airlines.org
http://www.airlines.org

For general information on aviation, contact
Federal Aviation Administration
800 Independence Avenue, SW
Washington, DC 20591-0001
Tel: 866-835-5322
http://jobs.faa.gov

For information on union representation for baggage and cargo handlers, contact
International Association of Machinists and Aerospace Workers
9000 Machinists Place
Upper Marlboro, MD 20772-2687
Tel: 301-967-4500
http://www.iamaw.org

Helicopter Pilots

OVERVIEW

Helicopter pilots serve in a wide range of fields from medicine to communications, and they are employed by both the government and private industry. They are vital in emergency situations, in gathering information, and in transporting people and cargo short distances. Helicopter pilots are employed across the United States and in other countries, and even in remote places throughout the world.

HISTORY

In the mid-1500s, the Italian inventor Leonardo da Vinci sketched a design of a flying vehicle that we now know as the helicopter. This design was impractical in full-sized form, and scientists and inventors experimented for the next three centuries to create a practical design for a flying vehicle. It was not until 1877 that Enrico Forlanini, an Italian engineer and professor, flew a steam-driven model helicopter for 20 seconds. Further experiments were attempted to increase flight time over the next few decades. With Orville and Wilbur Wright's groundbreaking flight of a fixed-wing aircraft on December 17, 1903, the modern age of aviation began. A Frenchmen named Louis Breguet constructed a helicopter that took a man aloft in 1907, but it was nearly three more decades before the first practical helicopter, the German Focke-Wulf 61, was produced in 1936. After World War II, great advances were made in the design and production of helicopters. They were used extensively in the Korean and Vietnam Wars to transport troops, supplies, and weapons. In the Vietnam War, helicopters were also heavily armed and used as gunships.

Helicopter pilots continue to play an important role in military operations today.

Today, helicopter pilots are counted on to perform a wide variety of tasks, including transporting sick and injured people to hospitals, reporting traffic conditions on radio and television news shows, and transporting workers and supplies to destinations that are inaccessible by other modes of transportation.

THE JOB

Helicopter pilots perform duties in medical evacuation, police and firefighting work, forestry, construction, communications, agriculture, and offshore oil exploration. They may serve as air taxis, carry workers and supplies to oil rigs, rescue stranded flood victims, lift heavy materials to work sites, fly patients from one hospital to another, or give news and traffic updates for the media. Many, but not all, helicopter pilots who do police work are also law enforcement officers. Their work includes traffic regulation and survey, vehicle pursuits, surveillance, patrol, and search.

In addition to flying, helicopter pilots keep records of their aircraft's engine performance and file flight plans. Before and after flying they check the aircraft for problems and may even do repairs and general upkeep on the craft if they are licensed to do so.

While flying, helicopter pilots must monitor several dials and gauges to make sure the aircraft is functioning properly. They monitor changes in pressure, fuel, and temperature. Helicopter pilots also navigate using landmarks, compasses, maps, and radio equipment.

REQUIREMENTS

High School

All prospective pilots must complete high school. A college preparatory curriculum is recommended because of the need for pilots to have at least some college education. Science and mathematics are two important subjects and you should also take advantage of any computer courses offered. You can start pursuing your pilot's license while in high school.

Postsecondary Training

Although helicopter pilots are not required to have a college degree, college credentials can lead to promotions and better jobs. Helicopter pilots may receive training in flying schools (which can be expensive) where they study the theory of flying, weather, radio, navigation, and Federal Aviation Administration (FAA) regulations. They also receive flight training.

Most of these pilots learn to fly as officers in the army. (For officers, a college degree is required.) To become licensed as a commercial helicopter pilot, a military pilot must pass the FAA military competency exam.

Certification or Licensing

To become a helicopter pilot, you must have a commercial pilot's license with a helicopter rating from the FAA. An applicant who is 18 years old and has 250 hours of flying time can apply for a commercial airplane pilot's license. In applying for this license, you must pass a rigid physical examination and a written test given by the FAA covering safe flight operations, federal aviation regulations, navigation principles, radio operation, and meteorology. You also must submit proof that the minimum flight-time requirements have been completed and, in a practical test, demonstrate flying skill and technical competence to a check pilot.

An instrument rating by the FAA and a restricted radiotelephone operator's permit by the Federal Communications Commission are required.

Other Requirements

Good judgment, emotional balance, and the ability to think and act under pressure are ideal personal characteristics for working as a helicopter pilot. To qualify, pilots must be at least 21 years of age and meet the physical requirements of employers.

EXPLORING

If you are interested in flying, join the (co-ed) Explorers (Boy Scouts of America) or a high school aviation club. At 16 years of age, you can start taking flying lessons. One of the most valuable experiences for high school students who want to be a pilot is to learn to be a ham radio operator, which is one of the qualifications for commercial flying.

EMPLOYERS

Helicopter pilots work for private companies and government agencies throughout the United States and the world. They can find work in the military and many industries, including agriculture, firefighting, police and public safety, mining, utilities, timber, broadcasting, and travel and tourism. Helicopter pilots also work for corporations, flight training schools, and for government agencies such as the FAA and the National Transportation Safety Board.

STARTING OUT

Most helicopter pilots receive their first job leads through the aviation schools where they received their training, federal and state employment agencies, private employment agencies, and job listings in the newspaper or on aviation industry-related Web sites.

ADVANCEMENT

Seniority, hours of flight time, and type of aircraft are the key factors in getting promotions in the helicopter industry. When starting out, most helicopter pilots fly the smaller, single-engine aircraft. As they gain experience and hours of flying time, they may fly larger helicopters and obtain higher paying jobs. Pilots employed by large companies may be promoted to chief pilot or aviation department manager.

EARNINGS

The rate of pay for helicopter pilots is based on level of experience, the size and type of craft, responsibilities, region, and employer. According to *Rotor & Wing's* 2006 helicopter industry salary survey, chief pilots in the civil government earned salaries ranging from $10,000 to $160,000 a year. Chief pilots in commercial settings earned from $10,000 to $360,000. Salaries also vary by specialty. Construction pilots earned an average of $68,400, law enforcement pilots earned $52,953, firefighting pilots earned $54,869, and offshore support pilots earned an average of $80,000 a year.

Median annual salaries for full-time commercial pilots (a category that includes helicopter pilots) were $65,340 in 2008, according to the U.S. Department of Labor. Salaries ranged from less than $32,020 to $129,580 or more.

Most employers of helicopter pilots provide medical, dental, and life insurance as well as paid vacations of about three weeks. For performing special services, such as flying to remote areas, they receive bonuses.

WORK ENVIRONMENT

Some helicopter pilots work overtime, extra hours, and both daytime and night shifts. The number of hours helicopter pilots work depends on the type of employment. Air taxi pilots and police helicopter pilots may work 40 hours a week. Those who do police work may work more than 40 hours a week. Agricultural, forestry, and fire pilots may also work long hours.

Inside helicopters, pilots must remain seated in the cramped space for hours at a time. There is often mental stress involved in the constant alertness and concentration necessary for monitoring the craft's gauges and reading instruments. Firefighting and law enforcement pilots are exposed to potential bodily harm while agricultural and construction pilots may be exposed to harsh chemicals.

OUTLOOK

The U.S. Department of Labor predicts that employment for aircraft pilots will grow about as fast as the average for all careers through 2018. There will be good opportunities in offshore oil support, emergency medical services, firefighting, and law enforcement. More jobs will be available in civil government and commercial transport than in corporate transport. Many employers are offering salary increases to keep qualified pilots.

FOR MORE INFORMATION

For information about industry publications, contact
AHS International—The Vertical Flight Society
217 North Washington Street
Alexandria, VA 22314-2538
Tel: 703-684-6777
E-mail: staff@vtol.org
http://www.vtol.org

For information on licensing, contact
Federal Aviation Administration
800 Independence Avenue, SW
Washington, DC 20591-0001
Tel: 866-835-5322
http://www.faa.gov

For information on careers and helicopter safety, contact
Helicopter Association International
1635 Prince Street
Alexandria VA 22314-2818
Tel: 703-683-4646
http://www.rotor.com

Industrial Traffic Managers

OVERVIEW

Industrial traffic managers handle the booking, billing, claims, and related paperwork for the safe and efficient movement of cargo by air, water, truck, or rail. They analyze the costs of different forms of transport and calculate the shipping rates for the customers. There are approximately 99,700 transportation, storage, and distribution managers employed in all industries in the United States. Industrial traffic managers are sometimes known as *supply chain managers*.

HISTORY

As the modes of transportation have improved over the centuries, so have the means of transporting freight from place to place. Businesses can now choose from among many alternatives—air, water, truck, or rail—to determine the best method for sending their goods. They want to find the method that will be the most efficient, economical, and reliable arrangement for each particular type of cargo. The job industrial traffic managers perform has helped add organization and efficiency to an increasingly complex process.

With the rise of mass production techniques in the 20th century, manufacturers have been able to produce more products than ever before. A company may produce hundreds of thousands of products each year, and each must reach its ultimate destination, the consumer. The vast numbers of products have created a need for people who specialize in seeing that

QUICK FACTS

School Subjects
Business
Mathematics

Personal Skills
Communication/ideas
Leadership/management

Work Environment
Primarily indoors
Primarily one location

Minimum Education Level
High school diploma

Salary Range
$45,320 to $79,000 to $130,020+

Certification or Licensing
Voluntary

Outlook
Decline

DOT
184

GOE
07.01.01, 09.08.01

NOC
0713

O*NET-SOC
11-3071.01, 43-5071.00

products are packed, shipped, and received properly and efficiently. Today's industrial traffic managers make use of the latest technological innovations to coordinate the shipping and receiving of products worldwide.

THE JOB

Industrial traffic managers direct and coordinate workers who document, classify, route, and schedule outgoing freight and who verify and reship incoming freight at warehouses and other work sites. They also quote rates and give other information to customers and handle customer complaints about damaged, missing, or overcharged goods. Some traffic managers decide which method of transportation of goods is best. They investigate different means of transportation and then make their decisions based on the efficiency and cost. Computers have made the traffic manager's job much easier. In order to make important judgments, traffic managers must make distance and rate calculations that can be done easily and quickly with computers. Computer programs, with their ability to analyze cost-effectiveness, can also help traffic managers decide on the most efficient means of transporting goods.

Traffic agents contact industrial and commercial firms to solicit freight business. These workers call on prospective shippers to explain the advantages of using their company's services. They quote tariff rates, schedules, and operating conditions, such as loading or unloading practices. When an agreement is reached, the traffic agent may also serve as liaison between the shipper and the carrier, help to settle complaints, or follow up on the handling of special goods, such as live animals, delicate equipment, or perishable goods. *Traffic clerks* keep records of incoming and outgoing freight by recording the destination, routing, weight, and tariffs. These workers may also be required to keep records of damaged freight and clients' claims of overcharge. *Shipping services sales representatives* perform similar work for parcel delivery businesses.

Rate supervisors analyze rates and routes in an effort to find ways to reduce transportation costs. They supervise the work of *traffic rate clerks*, who determine the rates that a transportation company will charge for shipping cargo of various kinds. *Freight rate analysts* also analyze rates, along with current and proposed government regulations, to determine how the transportation company should revise its rates and practices. These analysts also compile the shipping company's rate manual.

REQUIREMENTS

High School

Many jobs are available to high school graduates, especially with smaller companies, and part-time and summer employment is often available to high school students. You can prepare for a career as an industrial traffic manager by taking courses in economics, mathematics, science, and business administration.

Postsecondary Training

If you are interested in advancing to positions of greater responsibility, you are strongly advised to have at least some postsecondary education. More and more companies have begun to require one to two years of college education for entry into this field, especially when seeking employees interested in making a career with their company. Many community and junior colleges offer traffic and transportation curricula to prepare workers for employment as traffic agents and clerks. Some institutions combine course work with on-the-job experience in programs that lead to an associate's degree or a certificate of completion.

Certification or Licensing

The American Society of Transportation and Logistics offers the professional designation in logistics and supply chain management for entry-level workers in the field who are members of the organization and pass an examination. The society also offers the certified in transportation and logistics designation to applicants who are active members of the society and who have a four-year undergraduate degree or three years of professional experience. Applicants must pass exams in the following areas: general management principles and techniques, transportation economics and management, logistics management, and international transportation and logistics. They must also pass two of the following elective exam modules: creative component, logistics analysis, supply chain management, and logistics and supply chain strategy.

Other Requirements

Industrial traffic managers must be skilled in both verbal and written communication. They must be organized, responsible, dependable, and exacting with details. They must also be able to work easily with numerical data. Computer skills are often required for tracking the flow of goods.

EXPLORING

The best opportunity for experience in this field would be a part-time or summer job with a transportation company or a local moving company in a clerical capacity or as a truck helper. In these positions, you would be able to observe the work and responsibilities of traffic agents as well as talk with agents about their positions.

Work-experience programs provided by many companies permit you to get established with an employer as well as obtain valuable experience. You can also contact employers directly through letters of application.

EMPLOYERS

Approximately 99,700 transportation, storage, and distribution managers are employed in all industries in the United States. They work for all kinds of companies that oversee the transportation of their goods and materials.

STARTING OUT

Entry-level shipping and receiving positions generally do not require a high degree of educational achievement. Many positions are open to high school graduates, particularly in smaller companies. Management positions, however, are increasingly being filled by graduates of two-year college programs. Therefore, one of the best ways to find an entry-level position as an industrial traffic manager is to work with the career services office of the community or technical college at which you studied. You can also check newspaper want ads for job openings.

ADVANCEMENT

Many paths for advancement exist in this field. For example, someone entering the field as a rate and claims clerk might eventually be promoted to a position as a rate analyst. A routing clerk could be promoted to terminal cargo manager, and a company representative could advance to the position of traffic manager. Industrial traffic managers who earn a bachelor's degree in logistics might be promoted to the position of logistics manager.

EARNINGS

Starting salaries depend greatly on the applicant's level of education, college experience, other relevant work experience, and the degree of responsibility of the position. According to the U.S. Department of Labor, transportation, storage, and distribution managers had median annual earnings of $79,000 in 2008. The lowest paid 10 percent earned less than $45,320 annually. The most experienced industrial traffic managers, often those with a master's degree in business, earned $130,020 or more a year.

Fringe benefits vary widely, depending on the type and size of the company, although most will include vacations and holiday pay, health insurance plans, and in some cases, tuition reimbursement plans.

WORK ENVIRONMENT

Because of the diverse characteristics of each particular mode of transportation, it is difficult to make a general statement about working conditions. Some positions consist of outdoor work, others are almost exclusively indoors, and some are combinations of the two. The hours may be long or shift work may be required since some terminals operate around the clock and certain cargoes must be dispatched as soon as they arrive. Some positions, however, require only regular hours with weekends off.

OUTLOOK

Large and medium-sized companies are increasingly using computers to store and retrieve records. Computerized conveyor systems, robotics, and trucks, as well as scanners, are increasing productivity and eliminating the need for large numbers of workers. As a result, employment of industrial traffic managers is expected to decline slowly through 2018, according to the U.S. Department of Labor. Traffic management can never be completely computerized, however. Managers will still be needed to arrange and oversee shipments before they go out and when they arrive. Traffic clerks also will be affected by automation as most firms attempt to save money by using computerized tracking systems. Employment for these workers will grow more slowly than the average for all occupations through 2018.

FOR MORE INFORMATION

For information on certification, contact
American Society of Transportation and Logistics
PO Box 3363
Warrenton, VA 20188-1963
Tel: 202-580-7270
E-mail: info@astl.org
http://www.astl.org

For information on college programs and careers, visit the council's Web site.
Council of Supply Chain Management Professionals
333 East Butterfield Road, Suite 140
Lombard, IL 60148-6016
Tel: 630-574-0985
E-mail: cscmpadmin@cscmp.org
http://www.cscmp.org

For industry information, contact
Warehousing Education and Research Council
1100 Jorie Boulevard, Suite 170
Oak Brook, IL 60523-4423
Tel: 630-990-0001
E-mail: wercoffice@werc.org
http://www.werc.org

Visit the following Web site for more information about the field:
CAREERS in Supply Chain Management
http://www.careersinsupplychain.org

Military Pilots

OVERVIEW

Military pilots fly various types of specialized aircraft to transport troops and equipment and to execute combat missions. Military aircraft make up one of the world's largest fleets of specialized airplanes.

The U.S. Armed Forces are composed of five separate military services: the Army, Air Force, Marines, Navy, and Coast Guard (which is now part of the U.S. Department of Homeland Security). Pilots within these branches train, organize, and equip the nation's air services to support the national and international policies of the government.

Those who choose to join the U.S. Armed Forces dedicate their lives to protecting their fellow Americans. There are approximately 16,000 airplane pilots and 6,500 helicopter pilots in the military.

HISTORY

The age of modern aviation is generally considered to have begun with the famous flight of Orville and Wilbur Wright's heavier-than-air machine on December 17, 1903. On that day, the Wright brothers flew their machine four times and became the first airplane pilots.

Aviation developed rapidly as designers raced to improve upon the Wright brothers' design. During the early years of flight, many aviators earned a living as "barnstormers," entertaining people with stunts and by taking passengers on short flights around the countryside. Airplanes were quickly adapted to military use.

In 1907, the U.S. Army created an Aeronautical Division. Air power proved invaluable a few years later during World War I, bringing about major changes in military strategy. As a result, the United

QUICK FACTS

School Subjects
Computer science
Government
Physics

Personal Skills
Leadership/management
Technical/scientific

Work Environment
Indoors and outdoors
Primarily multiple locations

Minimum Education Level
Bachelor's degree

Salary Range
$31,863 to $68,277 to $176,263+

Certification or Licensing
None available

Outlook
About as fast as the average

DOT
378, 632

GOE
04.05.01

O*NET-SOC
55-1011.00, 55-2011.00, 55-3011.00, 55-3017.00

States began to assert itself as an international military power, and accordingly, the Army Air Service was created as an independent unit in 1918, although it remained under army direction for a time.

With Japan's surprise attack on Pearl Harbor in 1941, the United States was plunged into World War II. At its height, 13 million Americans fought in the different branches of the military services. When the war ended, the United States emerged as the strongest military power in the Western world. A large part of America's military success was due to the superiority of its air forces. Recognition of the strategic importance of air power led to the creation of the now wholly independent branch of service, the U.S. Air Force, in 1947. Two years later, the various branches of military service were unified under the Department of Defense (except the U.S. Coast Guard, which is overseen by the U.S. Department of Homeland Security).

Since then, military pilots have played an integral role during the Cold War, the Korean War, the Vietnam War, the Persian Gulf War, the War on Terrorism, and countless smaller skirmishes and engagements, as well as in noncombat and peacekeeping situations.

THE JOB

Military pilots operate many different jet and propeller planes. Aircraft range from combat airplanes and helicopters, to supersonic

A pilot navigates a U.S. Air Force F-15E Strike Eagle jet over Afghanistan during a mission. (*Staff Sergeant Aaron Allmon, U.S. Air Force*)

fighters and bombers. In addition to actually flying aircraft, military pilots are also responsible for developing flight plans; checking weather reports; briefing and directing all crew members; and performing system operation checks to test the proper functioning of instrumentation, controls, and electronic and mechanical systems on the flight deck. They also are responsible for coordinating their take-offs and landings with airplane dispatchers and air traffic controllers. At times, military pilots may be ordered to transport equipment and personnel, take reconnaissance photographs, spot and observe enemy positions, and patrol areas to carry out flight missions. After landing, military pilots must follow "afterlanding and shutdown" checklist procedures, and inform maintenance crews of any discrepancies or other problems noted during the flight. They must also present a written or oral flight report to their commanding officer.

There are several military aviation specialties. *Flight navigators* or *radar technicians* use radio, radar, and other equipment to help military pilots determine aircraft position and determine a route of travel. *Flight instructors* teach flight students how to fly via classroom training and in-flight instruction. *Test pilots* play an important role in the testing and development of new aircraft and related technologies. They are employed by aerospace companies, the National Aeronautics and Space Administration (NASA), and the U.S. military, primarily the air force and the navy. Combining knowledge of flying with a background in aeronautical engineering, they test new models of planes and make sure they function properly. Test pilots are sometimes called *research pilots, research test pilots,* and *experimental test pilots.*

The following paragraphs detail opportunities for military pilots in the five military branches.

Although the army is best known for its land-based occupations, it also employs military pilots to serve in combat, rescue, and reconnaissance settings. Army pilots are classified under the warrant officer designation along with other skilled experts in nonaviation related fields.

The air force has the largest number of military pilots. These pilots work in a variety of specialty areas including bombers, airlifts, special operations, surveillance, and navigation. Specific job titles in this branch of the military include *air battle managers, airlift pilots and navigators, bomber pilots and navigators, fighter pilots and navigators, reconnaissance/surveillance/electronic warfare pilots and navigators, special operations pilots and navigators,* and *tanker pilots and navigators.*

Marine aviation officers provide air support for ground troops during battle. They also transport equipment and personnel to various destinations.

Pilots in the navy are called *naval flight officers.* Unlike other military pilots, they take off and land their airplanes on both land bases and aircraft carriers. Depending on their specialty, they receive advanced training in air-to-air combat, bombing, search and rescue, aircraft carrier qualifications, over-water navigation, and low-level flying. Naval flight officer specialties include *turboprop maritime propeller pilots,* who track submarines, conduct surveillance, and gather photographic intelligence, and *helicopter pilots,* who search for underwater supplies, deliver supplies and personnel, and participate in emergency search-and-rescue missions.

The U.S. Coast Guard is the only armed force in the United States with domestic law enforcement authority. Its aviators enforce federal laws and treaties and conduct military operations to safeguard the American homeland.

REQUIREMENTS

High School

You will need at least a high school diploma in order to join the armed forces, and a college preparatory curriculum is recommended. High school courses in science, mathematics, physics, computers, and physical education will be the most helpful. It's also a good idea to take a foreign language. To enter the military, you must be at least 17 years old. Applicants who are age 17 must also have the consent of a parent or legal guardian.

Postsecondary Training

A four-year college degree is usually required to become a military pilot. Courses in engineering, meteorology, computer science, aviation law, business management, and military science are especially helpful. Physical education courses will also be important, as your physical health and endurance levels will constantly be challenged in the military.

There are several paths that you can choose from to get your postsecondary education. You may want to attend one of the four service academies: the U.S. Air Force Academy (for the air force), the U.S. Military Academy (for the army), the U.S. Naval Academy (for the navy and the Marines), or the U.S. Coast Guard Academy (for the coast guard). Competition to enter these institutions is intense. You will need to have a very strong academic background, involvement in community activities, and leadership experiences. Most applicants also need a nomination from an authorized source, which is usually a member of the U.S. Congress. If you choose one of these four academies, you will graduate with a bachelor's degree. You are then required to spend a minimum of five years on active duty, beginning as a junior officer.

Another option is to attend a four-year school that has a Reserve Officers' Training Corps (ROTC) program. Most state-supported colleges and universities have aviation programs, as do many private schools. Some schools focus solely on aviation education, such as Embry-Riddle Aeronautical University (http://www.erau.edu). Others, such as the University of North Dakota (http://www.aero.und.edu), are well known for their aviation and aerospace science programs.

Test pilots receive their training at civilian flight schools, such as the National Test Pilot School, or via military flight test schools (the U.S. Air Force Test Pilot School or the U.S. Naval Test Pilot School).

Each branch of the armed services has specific training requirements for its military pilots. Training in all branches will include flight simulation, classroom training, and basic flight instruction. For more information on specific requirements, contact a recruiter for the branch in which you are interested in entering.

Other Requirements

Stable physical and emotional health is essential for the aspiring pilot. Military pilots are expected to remain calm and levelheaded, no matter how stressful the situation. The physical requirements of this profession are very strict—you must have 20/20 vision with or without glasses, good hearing, normal heart rate and blood pressure, and no physical handicaps that could hinder performance.

You should have quick decision-making skills and reflexes to be a successful pilot. Decisiveness, self-confidence, good communication skills, and the ability to work well under pressure are also important personality traits. You should maintain an adaptable and flexible lifestyle, as your orders, missions, and station may change at any time.

Although military pilot careers are available to both men and women, some combat positions are only open to men.

EXPLORING

Military recruiters often visit high schools, so be sure to take advantage of this opportunity to learn more about this field. Take a tour of a military base or an aircraft carrier if you get the chance. Talk with family and friends who have served in the armed forces to get advice and information.

To get a real feel for what it's like to be a military pilot, check out one of several air combat schools that exist throughout the country. Through such programs, you can experience the cockpit of a fighter plane alongside an instructor, and even experience "dogfighting" in the sky. Air Combat USA, which is one such program, operates out of 30 airports nationwide. See the For More Information section at the end of this article to learn more.

EMPLOYERS

Military pilots are employed by the U.S. government. There are approximately 16,000 airplane pilots and 6,500 helicopter pilots in the military.

STARTING OUT

Once you've decided to become a military pilot, you should contact a military recruiter. The recruiter will help answer questions and suggest different options. To start out in any branch of the military, you must pass medical and physical tests, the Armed Services Vocational Aptitude Battery exam, and basic training. You must also sign an enlistment contract. This is a legal agreement that will bind you to a certain amount of military service, usually eight years. Active duty comprises two to six years of this agreement, and the remainder is normally spent in the reserves.

ADVANCEMENT

Each military branch has 10 officers' grades (O-1 through O-10) and five warrant officers' grades (W-1 through W-5). The higher the number, the more advanced a person's rank is. The various branches of the military have somewhat different criteria for promoting individuals; in general, however, promotions depend on factors such as length of time served, demonstrated abilities, recommendations, and scores on written exams. Promotions become more and more competitive as people advance in rank.

Military pilots may train for different aircraft and missions. Eventually, they may advance to senior officer or command positions. Military pilots with superior skills and training may advance to the position of *astronaut*. Astronauts pilot space vehicles on scientific and defense-related missions.

EARNINGS

The U.S. Congress sets the pay scales for the military after hearing recommendations from the president. The pay for equivalent grades is the same in all services (that is, anyone with a grade of O-4, for example, will have the same basic pay whether in the army, navy, Marines, air force, or coast guard). In addition to basic pay, personnel who frequently and regularly participate in combat may earn hazardous duty pay. Other special allowances include special duty pay and foreign duty pay. Earnings start relatively low but increase on a fairly regular basis as individuals advance in rank. When reviewing earnings, it is important to keep in mind that members of the military receive free housing, food, and health care—items that civilians typically pay for themselves.

All military pilots serve as officers in their respective branches. According to the Defense Finance and Accounting Service, officers starting out at a grade of O-1 received basic monthly pay of $2,655.30 in 2009. This would make for an annual salary of approximately $31,863.60. An officer with the grade O-5 and more than four years of experience earned $5,689.80 per month, or approximately $68,277.60 per year. And an officer with the top grade of O-10 and more than 20 years of experience had monthly basic earnings of $14,688.60, or approximately $176,263.20 annually.

Additional benefits for military personnel include uniform allowances, 30 days' paid vacation time per year, and the opportunity to retire after 20 years of service. Generally, those retiring will receive 40 percent of the average of the highest three years of their base pay. This amount rises incrementally, reaching 75 percent of the average of the highest three years of base pay after 30 years of service. All retirement provisions are subject to change, however, and you should verify them as well as current salary information before you enlist. Those who retire after 20 years of service are usually in their 40s and thus have plenty of time, as well as an accumulation of skills with which to start a second career.

WORK ENVIRONMENT

The work environment for military pilots is rewarding, varied, and sometimes stressful. Pilots may be assigned to one or more air bases around the world. They may take off and land on aircraft carriers, at conventional airports, in desert conditions under fierce fire from the enemy, or in countless other settings. They may fly the same routes for extended periods of time, but no two flights are ever the same. Military pilots can expect excitement and the chance to see the world, but they are responsible for the safety and protection of others.

OUTLOOK

The outlook for military workers, including military pilots, is expected to be excellent through 2018, according to the U.S. Department of Labor. While political and economic conditions will have an influence on the military's duties and employment outlook, it is a fact that the country will always need military pilots, both for defense and to protect its interests and citizens around the world. Only about 22,500 pilots are employed in the U.S. military, and only individuals with the highest achievement levels and skills will be able to serve as pilots. In addition to serving in the military, there are many more opportunities for pilots in other government agencies and in the private sector.

FOR MORE INFORMATION

For career information, visit the association's Web site.
Air Line Pilots Association, International
1625 Massachusetts Avenue, NW
Washington, DC 20036-2212
Tel: 703-689-2270
http://www.alpa.org

For information on licensing, contact
Federal Aviation Administration
800 Independence Avenue, SW
Washington, DC 20591-0001
Tel: 866-835-5322
http://www.faa.gov

For information on test pilots, contact
Society of Experimental Test Pilots
PO Box 986
Lancaster, CA 93584-0986
Tel: 661-942-9574
E-mail: Setp@setp.org
http://www.setp.org

To learn more about combat school experience, as well as pilot proficiency training, visit
Air Combat USA
http://www.aircombatusa.com

Read up on military news and developments by visiting
Defense-Aerospace.com
http://www.defense-aerospace.com

To get information on specific branches of the military, check out this site, which is the home of ArmyTimes.com, NavyTimes.com, AirForceTimes.com, and MarineCorpsTimes.com.
Military Times
http://www.militarytimes.com

Visit the following Web sites for information on test pilot schools:
National Test Pilot School
http://www.ntps.com

U.S. Air Force Test Pilot School
http://www.edwards.af.mil

U.S. Naval Test Pilot School
http://www.navair.navy.mil/USNTPS

If you're thinking of joining the armed forces, take a look at this site, which guides students and parents through the decision.
Today's Military
http://www.todaysmilitary.com

For information on becoming a military pilot, contact
United States Air Force
http://www.airforce.com

United States Army
http://www.goarmy.com

United States Coast Guard
http://www.gocoastguard.com

United States Marine Corps
http://www.marines.com

United States Navy
http://www.navy.com/officer/aviation

Pilots

QUICK FACTS

School Subjects
Mathematics
Physics

Personal Skills
Leadership/management
Technical/scientific

Work Environment
Primarily indoors
Primarily multiple locations

Minimum Education Level
Some postsecondary training

Salary Range
$55,330 to $111,680 to
$200,000+

Certification or Licensing
Required by all states

Outlook
About as fast as the average

DOT
196

GOE
07.03.01

NOC
2271

O*NET-SOC
53-2011.00, 53-2012.00

OVERVIEW

Pilots perform many different kinds of flying jobs. In general, pilots operate an aircraft for the transportation of passengers, freight, mail, or for other commercial purposes. There are approximately 116,000 civilian aircraft pilots and flight engineers employed in the United States.

HISTORY

The age of modern aviation is generally considered to have begun with the famous flight of Orville and Wilbur Wright's heavier-than-air machine on December 17, 1903. On that day, the Wright brothers flew their machine four times and became the first airplane pilots. In the early days of aviation, the pilot's job was quite different from that of the pilot of today. As he flew the first plane, for instance, Orville Wright was lying on his stomach in the middle of the bottom wing of the plane. There was a strap across his hips, and to turn the plane, Wright had to tilt his hips from side to side.

Aviation developed rapidly as designers raced to improve upon the Wright brothers' design. During the early years of flight, many aviators earned a living as "barnstormers," entertaining people with stunts and by taking passengers on short flights around the countryside. Airplanes were quickly adapted to military use. Pilots soon became famous for their war exploits and for feats of daring and endurance as improvements in airplane designs allowed them to make transcontinental, transoceanic, or transpolar flights. As airplanes grew more complex and an entire industry developed, pilots were joined by copilots and flight engineers to assist in operating the plane.

The airline industry originated from the U.S. government-run airmail service. Pilots who flew for this service were praised in newspapers, and their work in this new, advanced industry made their jobs seem glamorous. But during the Great Depression, pilots faced the threat of losing their high pay and status. The Air Line Pilots Association stepped in and won federal protection for the airline pilot's job. In 1978, when the airline industry was deregulated, many expected the pay and status of pilots to decrease. However, the steady growth of airlines built a demand for good pilots and their value remained high.

Today, pilots perform a variety of services. Many pilots fly for the military services. Pilots with commercial airlines fly millions of passenger and cargo flights each year. Other pilots use airplanes for crop dusting, pipeline and electric line inspection, skydiving, and advertising. Many pilots provide instruction for flight schools. A great many pilots fly solely for pleasure, and many people own their own small planes.

THE JOB

The best-known pilots are the commercial pilots who fly for the airlines. Responsible, skilled professionals, they are among the highest paid workers in the country. The typical pilot flight deck crew includes the *captain,* who is the pilot in command, and the *copilot,* or *first officer.* In larger aircraft, there may be a third member of the crew, called the *flight engineer,* or *second officer.* The captain of a flight is in complete command of the crew, the aircraft, and the passengers or cargo while they are in flight. In the air, the captain also has the force of law. The aircraft may hold 30 or 300 or more people or be completely loaded with freight, depending on the airline and type of operations. The plane may be fitted with either turbojet, turboprop (which are propellers driven by jet engines), or reciprocating propeller engines. An aircraft may operate near the speed of sound and at altitudes as high as 40,000 feet.

In addition to actually flying the aircraft, pilots must perform a variety of safety-related tasks. Before each flight, they must determine weather and flight conditions, ensure that sufficient fuel is on board to complete the flight safely, and verify the maintenance status of the aircraft. The captain briefs all crew members, including the flight attendants, about the flight. Pilots must also perform system operation checks to test the proper functioning of instrumentation, controls, and electronic and mechanical systems on the flight deck. Pilots coordinate their flight plan with airplane dispatchers and air traffic controllers. Flight plans include information about the airplane, the passenger or cargo load, and the air route the pilot is expected to take.

Once all pre-flight duties have been performed, the captain taxis the aircraft to the designated runway and prepares for takeoff. Takeoff speeds must be calculated based on the aircraft's weight. The aircraft systems, levers, and switches must be in proper position for takeoff. After takeoff, the pilots may engage an electrical device known as the autopilot. This device can be programmed to maintain the desired course and altitude. With or without the aid of the autopilot, pilots must constantly monitor the aircraft's systems.

Because pilots may encounter turbulence, emergencies, and other hazardous situations during a flight, good judgment and quick response are extremely important. Pilots receive periodic training and evaluation on their handling of in-flight abnormalities and emergencies and on their operation of the aircraft during challenging weather conditions. As a further safety measure, airline pilots are expected to adhere to checklist procedures in all areas of flight operations.

During a flight, pilots monitor aircraft systems, keep a watchful eye on local weather conditions, perform checklists, and maintain constant communication with the air traffic controllers along the flight route. The busiest times for pilots are during takeoff and landing. The weather conditions at the aircraft's destination must be obtained and analyzed. The aircraft must be maneuvered and properly configured to make a landing on the runway. When the cloud cover is low and visibility is poor, pilots rely solely on the instruments on the flight deck. These instruments include an altimeter and an artificial horizon. Pilots select the appropriate radio navigation frequencies and corresponding course for the ground-based radio and microwave signals that provide horizontal, and in some cases vertical, guidance to the landing runway.

After the pilots have safely landed the aircraft, the captain taxis it to the ramp or gate area where passengers and cargo are off-loaded. Pilots then follow "afterlanding and shutdown" checklist procedures, and inform maintenance crews of any discrepancies or other problems noted during the flight.

Pilots must also keep detailed logs of their flight hours, both for payroll purposes and to comply with Federal Aviation Administration (FAA) regulations. Pilots with major airlines generally have few non-flying duties. Pilots with smaller airlines, charter services, and other air service companies may be responsible for loading the aircraft, refueling, keeping records, performing minor repairs and maintenance, and arranging for major repairs.

An airline pilot readies a Boeing 737 for takeoff. (*Diether Endlicher, AP Photo*)

The *chief pilot* directs the operation of the airline's flight department. This individual is in charge of training new pilots, preparing schedules and assigning flight personnel, reviewing their performance, and improving their morale and efficiency. Chief pilots make sure that all legal and government regulations affecting flight operations are observed, advise the airline during contract negotiations with the pilots' union, and handle a multitude of administrative details.

In addition to airline pilots, there are various other types of pilots. *Business pilots,* or *executive pilots,* fly for businesses that have their own planes. These pilots transport cargo, products, or people and maintain the company's planes as well. *Test pilots,* though there are not many, are very important. Combining knowledge of flying with an engineering background, they test new models of planes and make sure they function properly. *Flight instructors* are pilots who teach others how to fly. They teach in classrooms or provide in-flight instruction. Other pilots work as *examiners,* or *check pilots.* They fly with experienced pilots as part of their periodic review; they may also give examinations to pilots applying for licenses.

Some pilots are employed in specialties, such as *photogramme-try pilots,* who fly planes or helicopters over designated areas and photograph the earth's surface for mapping and other purposes. *Facilities-flight-check pilots* fly specially equipped planes to test air navigational aids, air traffic controls, and communications equipment and to evaluate installation sites for such equipment.

REQUIREMENTS

High School

All prospective pilots must complete high school. A college preparatory curriculum is recommended because of the need for pilots to have at least some college education. Science and mathematics are two important subjects and you should also take advantage of any computer courses offered. You can start pursuing your pilot's license while in high school.

Postsecondary Training

Most companies that employ pilots require at least two years of college training; many require applicants to be college graduates. Courses in engineering, meteorology, physics, and mathematics are helpful in preparing for a pilot's career. Flying can be learned in either military or civilian flying schools. There are approximately 600 civilian flying schools certified by the FAA, including some colleges and universities that offer degree credit for pilot training. Pilots leaving the military are in great demand.

According to the U.S. Department of Labor, "initial training for airline pilots typically includes a week of company indoctrination; three to six weeks of ground school and simulator training; and 25 hours of initial operating experience, including a check-ride with an FAA aviation safety inspector."

Certification or Licensing

To become a pilot, certain rigid training requirements must be met. Although obtaining a private pilot's license is not difficult, it may be

On the Web

AvJobs.com
http://www.avjobs.com

Cleared to Dream
http://www.clearedtodream.org

Experimental Aircraft Association
http://www.eaa.org

Let's Go Flying!
http://www.aopa.org/letsgoflying

quite difficult to obtain a commercial license. If you are 16 or over and can pass the rigid mandatory physical examination, you may apply for permission to take flying instruction. This instruction consists of classroom education and flight training from a FAA-certified flight instructor.

Before you make your first solo flight, you must get a medical certificate (certifying that you are in good health) and an instructor-endorsed student pilot certificate. In order to get the student pilot certificate, you must pass a test given by the flight instructor. This test will have questions about FAA rules as well as questions about the model and make of the aircraft you will fly. If you pass the test and the instructor feels you are prepared to make a solo flight, the instructor will sign—or endorse— your student pilot certificate and logbook.

To apply for a private pilot's license, you must take a written examination. To qualify for it, you must be at least 17 years of age, successfully fulfill a solo flying requirement of 20 hours or more, and meet instrument flying and cross-country flying requirements.

All pilots and copilots must be licensed by the FAA before they can do any type of commercial flying. An applicant who is 18 years old and has 250 hours of flying time can apply for a commercial airplane pilot's license. In applying for this license, you must pass a rigid physical examination and a written test given by the FAA covering safe flight operations, federal aviation regulations, navigation principles, radio operation, and meteorology. You also must submit proof that the minimum flight-time requirements have been completed and, in a practical test, demonstrate flying skill and technical competence to a check pilot. Before you receive an FAA license, you must also receive a rating for the kind of plane you can fly (single-engine, multiengine, or seaplane) and for the specific type of plane, such as Boeing 707 or 747.

All airline pilots who are paid to transport passengers must have an airline transport pilot's license issued by the FAA. To obtain this license, pilots must be at least 23 years of age, have accrued at least 1,500 hours of flying experience (including night and instrument flying), pass FAA written and flight examinations, and have one or more advanced equipment ratings.

An instrument rating by the FAA and a restricted radiotelephone operator's permit by the Federal Communications Commission are required. All airline captains must have an air transport pilot license. Applicants for this license must be at least 23 years old and have a minimum of 1,500 hours of flight time, including night flying and instrument time. All pilots are subject to two-year flight reviews, regular six-month FAA flight checks, simulator tests, and medical exams. The FAA also makes unannounced spot-check inspections of all pilots.

Jet pilots, helicopter pilots, and agricultural pilots all have special training in their respective fields.

Additionally, airline pilots who complete rigorous training and background screening are deputized as federal law enforcement officers and are issued firearms. This training prepares them to protect the cockpit against hijackers and intruders, if necessary.

Other Requirements

Sound physical and emotional health are essential requirements for aspiring pilots. Emotional stability is necessary because the safety of other people depends upon a pilot remaining calm and level-headed, no matter how trying the situation. Physical health is equally important. You must have 20/20 vision with or without glasses, good hearing, normal heart rate and blood pressure, and no physical handicaps that could hinder performance.

EXPLORING

High school students who are interested in flying may join the (co-ed) Explorers (Boy Scouts of America) or a high school aviation club. At 16 years of age, you may start taking flying lessons. One of the most valuable experiences for high school students who want to be a pilot is to learn to be a ham radio operator, which is one of the qualifications for commercial flying.

EMPLOYERS

There are approximately 116,000 commercial pilots in the United States. The commercial airlines, including both passenger and cargo transport companies, are the primary employers of pilots. Pilots also work in general aviation, and many are trained and employed by the military.

STARTING OUT

A large percentage of commercial pilots have received their training in the armed forces. A military pilot who wants to apply for a commercial airplane pilot's license is required to pass only the Federal Aviation Regulations examination if application is made within a year after leaving the service.

Pilots possessing the necessary qualifications and license may apply directly to a commercial airline for a job. If accepted, they will go through a company orientation course, usually including both classroom instruction and practical training in company planes.

Those who are interested in becoming business pilots will do well to start their careers in mechanics. They may also have military flying experience, but the strongest recommendation for a business pilot's job is an airframe and power plant (A and P) rating. They should also have at least 500 hours of flying time and have both commercial and instrument ratings on their license. Job-seekers may apply directly to the firm for which they would like to work.

ADVANCEMENT

Many beginning pilots start out as copilots. Seniority is the pilot's most important asset. If pilots leave one employer and go to another, they must start from the bottom again, no matter how much experience was gained with the first employer. The position of captain on a large airline is a high-seniority, high-prestige, and high-paying job. Pilots may also advance to the position of check pilot, testing other pilots for advanced ratings; chief pilot, supervising the work of other pilots; or to administrative or executive positions with a commercial airline (ground operations). They may also become self-employed, opening a flying business, such as a flight instruction, agricultural aviation, air taxi, or charter service.

EARNINGS

Airline pilots are among the highest paid workers in the country. Salaries vary widely depending on a number of factors, including the specific airline, type of aircraft flown, number of years with a company, and level of experience. Airline pilots are also paid more for international and nighttime flights.

The U.S. Department of Labor reports that mean annual earnings of airline pilots and copilots employed in scheduled air transportation were $111,680 in 2008. The lowest paid 10 percent of all pilots earned less than $55,330. Very experienced pilots at large commercial airlines may make $200,000 or more annually.

Pilots with commercial airlines receive life and health insurance and retirement benefits; if they fail their FAA physical exam during their career, they are eligible to receive disability benefits. Some airlines give pilots allowances for buying and cleaning their uniforms.

Pilots and their families usually fly free or at reduced fares on their own or other airlines.

WORK ENVIRONMENT

Airline pilots work with the best possible equipment and under highly favorable circumstances. They command a great deal of respect. Although many pilots regularly fly the same routes, no two flights are ever the same. FAA regulations limit airline pilots to no more than 100 flying hours per month (or 1,000 hours a year). Most airline pilots fly approximately 65–75 hours per month and spend at least another 65–75 hours a month on nonflying duties.

While being an airline pilot can be a rewarding career, it can also be extremely stressful. During flights, they must maintain constant concentration on a variety of factors. They must always be alert to changes in conditions and to any problems that may occur. They are often responsible for hundreds of lives besides their own, and they are always aware that flying contains an element of risk. During emergencies, they must react quickly, logically, and decisively. Pilots often work irregular hours, may be away from home a lot, and are subject to jet lag and other conditions associated with flying. Pilots employed with smaller airlines may also be required to perform other, nonflying duties, which increase the number of hours they work each month.

For other pilots who handle small planes, emergency equipment, and supply delivery or routes to remote and isolated areas, the hazards may be more evident. Dropping medical supplies in Central Africa, flying relief supplies into war zones, or delivering mail to northern Alaska are more difficult tasks than most pilots face. Business pilot schedules may be highly irregular and they must be on call for a great portion of their off-duty time. Business pilots and most private and small plane pilots are also frequently called upon to perform maintenance and repairs.

Today, even commercial pilots face dangers that rival those encountered by small-plane pilots in war-torn or hard-to-reach areas. Airplanes have been a favorite target for terrorist activity for a number of years because they provide easy access to large numbers of hostages and transportation anywhere in the world. In September 2001, terrorists found it easy to board commercial flights, take command, and kill pilots, air crew, passengers, and huge numbers of workers at New York's World Trade Center and the Pentagon. Since then, all kinds of safety and security measures have been implemented at airports and on board aircraft. Engineers are designing ways to secure cockpits to protect pilots and crew, as well as ways to communicate dangers to ground crew. Even so, flying an aircraft carries risks that are on the minds of all pilots today.

OUTLOOK

The U.S. Department of Labor predicts that employment for pilots will grow about as fast as the average for all careers through 2018. The entire airline industry has slowed. More than 100,000 airline employees were laid off after the 2001 terrorist attacks. To keep from going bankrupt, many airlines will undergo restructuring that will involve more layoffs and hiring freezes.

The airline industry expects a slow recovery process. It will take some time for crew and passengers to become accustomed to heightened security procedures and for traveler confidence to return. To compound problems, the airline industry is extremely sensitive to changes in the economy. When the economy suffers a downturn, everyone is less likely to spend money on air travel.

Opportunities will be best at regional airlines and low-fare carriers, which have experienced faster growth than the major airlines. Pilots who fly for air cargo carriers will also have good opportunities as these companies receive more shipping business as a result of security restrictions on the shipping of freight via passenger airlines. Employment for flight engineers is expected to decline as more planes are built that require only two-person crews.

FOR MORE INFORMATION

For career information, visit the association's Web site.
Air Line Pilots Association, International
1625 Massachusetts Avenue, NW
Washington, DC 20036-2212
Tel: 703-689-2270
http://www.alpa.org

To read The Airline Handbook, *visit the ATAA Web site.*
Air Transport Association of America (ATAA)
1301 Pennsylvania Avenue, NW, Suite 1100
Washington, DC 20004-1738
Tel: 202-626-4000
E-mail: ata@airlines.org
http://www.airlines.org

For information on experimental aircraft, contact
Experimental Aircraft Association
EAA Aviation Center
3000 Poberezny Road
Oshkosh, WI 54902-8939

Tel: 920-426-4800
http://www.eaa.org

For more information about the history of the FAA, pilot schools, and licensing, contact
Federal Aviation Administration (FAA)
800 Independence Avenue, SW
Washington, DC 20591-0001
Tel: 866-835-5322
http://www.faa.gov

For information on careers and helicopter safety, contact
Helicopter Association International
1635 Prince Street
Alexandria VA 22314-2818
Tel: 703-683-4646
http://www.rotor.com

For information on test pilots, contact
Society of Experimental Test Pilots
PO Box 986
Lancaster, CA 93584-0986
Tel: 661-942-9574
E-mail: Setp@setp.org
http://www.setp.org

For information on career opportunities for women in aviation, contact
Women in Aviation International
Morningstar Airport
3647 State Route 503 South
West Alexandria, OH 45381-9354
Tel: 937-839-4647
http://www.wai.org

INTERVIEW

Robert Szablak is a captain with American Airlines. He has worked in the aviation industry for approximately 37 years. He discussed his career with the editors of Careers in Focus: Aviation.

Q. What planes do you fly? Can you describe your typical schedule?

A. Currently I am flying the Boeing 757 and 767 although I have flown many other aircraft since starting to fly professionally in 1972 and while in the learning/training process since 1968. Typically I fly in the United States, Canada, and some European destinations. My schedule varies every month, but usually I work about 15 days [per] month. In our current aviation environment there may be several other days that I may be involved in our profession doing other duties. These may include reviewing airline and aircraft manuals and aviation-type revisions and updates, mentorship and community services, and just spending time enjoying your career, the airport, your family, and your many friends who enjoy flying and the airport.

Q. What made you want to become a pilot?

A. From a very early age, about two or three years old, my parents took me to the airport. This was about 1956 and I believe my parents were also quite interested in the airport. They were not involved with working out there, but the times made it a very interesting place to be. I initially just wanted to work out there. I enjoyed the airlines, schedules, routes each carrier flew, watching the people traveling, and the environment in general. The flying/pilot part, I would estimate, started at about age 10. I thought it would be very exciting to play a part in getting people to their destinations safely and professionally. As I got older I really began to learn what the concept of professionally flying an aircraft meant. The responsibility and commitment required to this career is tremendous. I enjoyed fast and slow aircraft of all kinds, the different airports, the travel and the destinations, the people that you would meet, and all the benefits of flying and working at the finest airline in the world. I hope that your readers realize that I did *not* believe that pay and travel benefits were my main reasons for wanting to be a pilot. A pilot does, in most cases, get paid fairly well, but it takes some time and you will earn every dime that you make! I believe flying anything from a Piper Cub to a Boeing 777 is a wonderful and gratifying experience.

Q. How did you get your first job as a pilot?

A. I got my first job in the aviation industry in Rochester, New York. I received flight training in high school and at the local airport. I believe your flight training and the planning of your career in aviation is a very interesting subject. I had dreams of flying in the military, as a corporate pilot, and my obvious choice was at an airline. The process of making any of those choices happen is not easy and you need plenty of ability, commitment, some luck, and a lot of help and advice. You can do just about everything correctly, but that does not ensure you will get the job you want. There are many things you need to do right, but I have always said flying skills, interest in your career, and having the ability to communicate with others are very important.

My first job was as a flight instructor. After training at this school and receiving numerous flying ratings I was offered a job as a flight instructor. This job taught basics in teaching flying, communication, and dealing with your fellow aviators. I enjoyed and encourage others to become certified flight instructors during their career at one time—preferably in the beginning.

Q. What are some of the pros and cons of work as a pilot?

A. I believe having the ability to be at the airport and flying all over the world is a big positive. You could be stuck in an office somewhere with no windows. I also think this career makes most pilots proud and very complete people. The requirements for professionalism, commitment, and responsibility should make one a happy and content person. The ability to travel and see other cultures, different scenery, work with others, and know you have made a difference in your life and possibly a few others makes me feel satisfied and happy. I also like the interaction with others. I am happy to be around all the other people at the airport. I enjoy seeing other pilots, flight attendants, ticket agents, talking with dispatchers, passengers, and even the people working in the airport restaurant and barbershop. I know not everyone feels this way but it just happens to be my personality and I feel that those people and the airport enhance my outlook and attitude.

I do not feel there are very many bad things about my job. There are some things out there that may be considered less enjoyable. They may include long days, time zone changes, altered sleep patterns, bad weather, airport delays, and the stresses that come with some passengers and the business environment. Everyone who works at the airport has the same life issues and challenges that make all of our lives more and more interesting. Pilots are generally very fair, flexible, compassionate, and determined.

I believe that there are a whole lot more pros than cons while working at the airport as a pilot. For most pilots the day you are not flying, for whatever reason, is the day that you will realize just how fortunate that you were. Many people do not realize all the good things that they have until they are gone!

Q. What advice would you give to young people who want to become pilots?

A. There is a lot of advice I could give to students about this career. The first would be to get a good education. Work well with others. Try to maintain your health, and be careful in the life that you lead. Start your flying training early and realize that you will need to do a lot of things correctly in school and in your flying ambitions. You should realize that it takes a big commitment to pursue a flying career. This applies to civilian and military flying in preparation for a professional pilot career at an airline. Drugs, drinking, and doing dumb things in your life or others people's lives do not enhance you chances of flying airplanes as your chosen profession. Do the right thing when it comes to yourself and others; it will get noticed and will be appreciated. Find a mentor, and try to really talk with him or her when possible. This should not always include text messaging, Twittering, cell phones, and the reliance of only e-mailing. Talk to people, learn from people, and develop a real personality and an ability to communicate with others. This will enhance your speaking abilities and communication skills. This will help make you a well-rounded person, increase your motivation, and be a great captain and aviator.

Reservation and Ticket Agents

QUICK FACTS

School Subjects
Business
Computer science
English

Personal Skills
Communication/ideas
Helping/teaching

Work Environment
Primarily indoors
Primarily one location

Minimum Education Level
Some postsecondary training

Salary Range
$19,180 to $34,420 to
$48,250+

Certification or Licensing
None available

Outlook
About as fast as the average

DOT
238

GOE
11.03.01

NOC
6433

O*NET-SOC
43-4181.00, 43-4181.01,
43-4181.02

OVERVIEW

Reservation and ticket agents are employed by airlines, bus companies, railroads, and cruise lines to help customers in several ways. *Reservation agents* make and confirm travel arrangements for passengers by using computers and manuals to determine timetables, taxes, and other information.

Ticket agents sell tickets in terminals or in separate offices. Like reservation agents, they also use computers and manuals containing scheduling, boarding, and rate information to plan routes and calculate ticket costs. They determine whether seating is available, answer customer inquiries, check baggage, and direct passengers to proper places for boarding. They may also announce arrivals and departures and assist passengers in boarding. There are approximately 104,270 reservation and ticket agents employed in the scheduled air transportation industry in the United States.

HISTORY

Since the earliest days of commercial passenger transportation (by boat or stagecoach), someone has been responsible for making sure that space is available and that everyone on board pays the proper fare. As transportation grew into a major industry over the years, the job of making reservations and selling tickets became a specialized occupation.

The airline industry experienced its first boom in the early 1930s. By the end of that decade, millions of people were flying each year. Since the introduction of passenger-carrying jet planes in 1958, the number of people traveling by air has multiplied many times over. The majority of reservation and ticket agents now work for airlines.

A number of innovations have helped make the work of reservation and ticket agents easier and more efficient. The introduction of automated telephone services allows customers to check on flight availability and arrival/departure times without having to wait to speak to an agent. Computers have both simplified the agents' work and put more resources within their reach. Since the 1950s, many airlines have operated computerized scheduling and reservation systems, either individually or in partnership with other airlines. Until recently, these systems were not available to the general consumer. In the last decade, however, the growth of the Internet has permitted travelers to access scheduling and rate information, make reservations, and purchase tickets without contacting an agent. Additionally, electronic tickets have largely replaced the traditional paper ticket. Despite these innovations, there will always be a need for reservation and ticketing agents, primarily for safety and security purposes. These employees still fill a vital role in the transportation industry.

A gate agent answers a customer's question. (*David R. Frazier, The Image Works*)

THE JOB

Airline reservation agents are sales agents who work in large central offices run by airline companies. Their primary job is to book and confirm reservations for passengers on scheduled flights. At the request of the customer or a ticket agent, they plan the itinerary and other travel arrangements. While many agents still use timetables, airline manuals, reference guides, and tariff books, most of this work is performed using specialized computer programs.

Computers are used to make, confirm, change, and cancel reservations. After asking for the passenger's destination, desired travel time, and airport of departure, reservation agents type the information into a computer and quickly obtain information on all flight schedules and seating availability. If the plane is full, the agent may suggest an alternative flight or check to see if space is available on another airline that flies to the same destination. Agents may even book seats on competing airlines, especially if their own airline can provide service on the return trip.

Reservation agents answer telephone inquiries about such things as schedules, fares, arrival and departure times, and cities serviced by their airline. They may maintain an inventory of passenger space available so they can notify other personnel and ticket stations of changes and try to book all flights to capacity. Some reservation agents work in more specialized areas, handling calls from travel agents or booking flights for members of frequent flyer programs. Agents working with international airlines must also be informed of visa regulations and other travel developments. This information is usually supplied by the *senior reservation agent,* who supervises and coordinates the activities of the other agents.

General transportation ticket agents for any mode of travel (air, bus, rail, or ship) sell tickets to customers at terminals or at separate ticket offices. Like reservation agents, they book space for customers. In addition, they use computers to prepare bookings, calculate fares, and collect payment. At the terminals they check and tag luggage, direct passengers to the proper areas for boarding, keep records of passengers on each departure, and help with customer problems, such as lost baggage or missed connections. *Airline ticket agents* may have additional duties, such as paging arriving and departing passengers and finding accommodations or new travel arrangements for passengers in the event of flight cancellations.

In airports, *gate agents* assign seats, issue boarding passes, make public address announcements of departures and arrivals, and help elderly or disabled passengers board the planes. In addition, they may also provide information to disembarking passengers about ground transportation, connecting flights, and local hotels.

Regardless of where they work, reservation and transportation ticket agents must be knowledgeable about their companies' policies and procedures, as well as the standard procedures of their industry. They must be aware of the availability of special promotions and services and be able to answer any questions customers may have.

REQUIREMENTS

High School

Reservation and ticket agents are generally required to have at least a high school diploma. Applicants should be able to type and must have good communication and problem-solving skills. Because computers are being used more and more in this field, you should have a basic knowledge of computers and computer software. Previous experience working with the public is also helpful for the job. Knowledge of geography and foreign languages are other valuable skills, especially for international service agents.

Postsecondary Training

Some college is preferred, although it is not considered essential for the job. Some colleges now offer courses specifically focused on ticket reservations.

Reservation agents receive classroom instruction that lasts several weeks to a month. They are taught how to read schedules, calculate fares, and plan itineraries. They learn how to use computer programs to get information and reserve space efficiently. They also study company policies and government regulations that apply to the industry.

Transportation ticket agents receive less training, consisting of about one week of classroom instruction. They learn how to read tickets and schedules, assign seats, and tag baggage. This is followed by one week of on-the-job training, working alongside an experienced agent. After mastering the simpler tasks, the new ticket agents are trained to reserve space, make out tickets, and handle the boarding gate.

Other Requirements

Because you will be in constant contact with the public, professional appearance, a clear and pleasant speaking voice, and a friendly personality are important qualities. You need to be tactful in keeping telephone time to a minimum without alienating your customers. In addition, you should enjoy working with people, have a good memory, and be able to maintain your composure when working with harried or unhappy travelers. Agents form a large part of the public image of their company.

Although not a requirement, many agents belong to labor unions, such as the Transport Workers Union of America and the International Brotherhood of Teamsters.

EXPLORING

You may wish to apply for part-time or summer work with transportation companies in their central offices or at terminals. A school counselor can help you arrange an information interview with an experienced reservation and transportation ticket agent. Talking to an agent directly about his or her duties can help you to become more familiar with transportation operations.

EMPLOYERS

Reservation and ticket agents employed in scheduled air transportation hold approximately 104,270 jobs in the United States. In addition to working for commercial airlines, they also work for other transportation companies, such as rail, ship, and bus lines.

STARTING OUT

To find part-time or summer work, apply directly to the personnel or employment offices of transportation companies. Ask your school counselor or college career services director for information about job openings, requirements, and possible training programs. Additionally, contact transportation unions for lists of job openings.

ADVANCEMENT

With experience and a good work record, some reservation and ticket agents can be promoted to supervisory positions. They can also become city and district sales managers for ticket offices. Beyond this, opportunities for advancement are limited. However, achieving seniority within a company can give an agent the first choice of shifts and available overtime.

EARNINGS

According to the U.S. Department of Labor, reservation and transportation ticket agents employed in scheduled air transportation earned mean salaries of $34,420 in 2008. Salaries for all reservation and ticket agents ranged from less than $19,180 per year, while the highest paid 10 percent earned more than $48,250 annually.

Most agents can earn overtime pay; many employers also pay extra for night work. Benefits vary according to the place of work, experience, and union membership; however, most receive vacation and sick pay, health insurance, and retirement plans. Agents, especially those employed by the airlines, often receive free or reduced-fare transportation for themselves and their families.

WORK ENVIRONMENT

Reservation and ticket agents generally work 40 hours per week. Approximately 14 percent of workers in this field are employed part time. Those working in reservations typically work in cubicles with their own computer terminals and telephone headsets. They are often on the telephone and at their computers all day long. Conversations with customers and computer activity may be monitored and recorded by their supervisors for evaluation and quality reasons. Agents might also be required to achieve sales or reservations quotas. During holidays or when special promotions and discounts are being offered, agents are especially busy. At these times or during periods of severe weather, passengers may become difficult. Handling customer frustrations can be stressful, but agents must maintain composure and a pleasant manner when speaking with customers.

Ticket agents working in airports face a busy and noisy environment. They may stand most of the day and lift heavy objects such as luggage and packages. During holidays and busy times, their work can become extremely hectic as they process long lines of waiting customers. Storms and other factors may delay or even cancel flights. Like reservation agents, ticket agents may be confronted with upset passengers, but must be able to maintain composure at all times.

OUTLOOK

According to the U.S. Department of Labor, employment for reservation and ticket agents is expected grow about as fast as the average for all occupations through 2018. Technology is changing the way consumers purchase tickets. "Ticketless" travel, or automated reservations ticketing, has reduced the need for agents. In addition, many airports now have computerized kiosks that allow passengers to reserve and purchase tickets themselves. Passengers can also access information about fares and flight times on the Internet, where they can also make reservations and purchase tickets. However, for security reasons, all of these services cannot be fully automated, so the need for reservation and transportation ticket agents will never be completely eliminated.

Most openings will occur as experienced agents transfer to other occupations or retire. Competition for jobs is fierce due to declining demand, low turnover, and because of the glamour and attractive travel benefits associated with the industry.

Overall, the transportation industry will remain heavily dependent on the state of the economy. During periods of recession or public fear about the safety of air travel, passenger travel generally declines and transportation companies are less likely to hire new workers, or may even resort to layoffs.

FOR MORE INFORMATION

For industry and statistical information, as well as to read The Airline Handbook *online, visit the association's Web site.*
Air Transport Association of America
1301 Pennsylvania Avenue, NW, Suite 1100
Washington, DC 20004-1738
Tel: 202-626-4000
E-mail: ata@airlines.org
http://www.airlines.org

For information on the airline industry, contact
Federal Aviation Administration
800 Independence Avenue, SW
Washington, DC 20591-0001
Tel: 866-835-5322
http://www.faa.gov

Travel Agents

OVERVIEW

Travel agents assist individuals or groups who will be traveling by planning their itineraries, making transportation, hotel, and tour reservations, obtaining or preparing tickets, and performing related services. There are approximately 105,000 travel agents employed in the United States.

HISTORY

The first travel agency in the United States was established in 1872. Before this time, travel as an activity was not widespread, due to wars and international barriers, inadequate transportation and hotels, lack of leisure, the threat of contagious disease, and lower standards of living. Despite the glamour attached to such early travelers as Marco Polo, people of the Middle Ages, and of the 17th and 18th centuries were not accustomed to traveling for pleasure.

The manufacturing operations that started in the industrial revolution caused international trade to expand greatly. Commercial traffic between countries stimulated both business and personal travel. Yet until the 20th century, travel was arduous, and most areas were unprepared for tourists.

The travel business began with Thomas Cook, an Englishman who first popularized the guided tour. In 1841, Cook arranged his first excursion—a special Midland Counties Railroad Company train to carry passengers from Leicester to a temperance meeting in Loughborough. His business grew rapidly. He made arrangements for 165,000 visitors to attend

QUICK FACTS

School Subjects
Business
Computer science
Geography

Personal Skills
Communication/ideas
Helping/teaching

Work Environment
Indoors and outdoors
One location with some travel

Minimum Education Level
High school diploma

Salary Range
$18,770 to $30,570 to $65,000+

Certification or Licensing
Voluntary (certification)
Required by certain states (licensing)

Outlook
Little or no growth

DOT
252

GOE
10.03.01

NOC
6431

O*NET-SOC
41-3041.00

the Great Exhibition of 1851 in London. The following year, he organized the first "Cook's Tour." Earnest groups of English tourists were soon seen traveling by camel to view the Pyramids and the Sphinx, gliding past historic castles on the Rhine, and riding by carriage to view the wonders of Paris. The "Grand Tour" of Europe soon became an integral part of a young person's education among the privileged classes.

In the next hundred years, the development of the railroads, the replacement of sailing ships with faster steamships, the advent of the automobile and the bus, and the invention of the airplane provided an improved quality of transportation that encouraged people to travel for relaxation and personal enrichment. At the same time, cities, regions, and countries began to appreciate the economic aspects of travel. Promotional campaigns were organized to attract and accommodate tourists. Formal organization of the travel industry was reflected in the establishment in 1931 of the American Society of Travel Agents (ASTA).

Most airlines and other travel suppliers now offer consumers the option of making their own travel arrangements through online reservation services, readily accessible through the Internet. With this as an option, travelers are becoming less dependent upon agents to make travel arrangements for them. Travel agents have responded to this development by focusing on niche markets (such as foreign visitors to the United States) and specializing in certain locales or travel options. Additionally, nearly all travel agents use the Internet to conduct research and book trips for customers.

In the past decade, travel has become less expensive and more people are traveling for business and pleasure. As long as travel continues to grow in popularity, there will be a need for travel agents to help people plan their vacations wisely.

THE JOB

The travel agent may work as a salesperson, travel consultant, tour organizer, travel guide, bookkeeper, or small business executive. If the agent operates a one-person office, he or she usually performs all of these functions. Other travel agents work in offices with dozens of employees, which allows them to specialize in certain areas. In such offices, one staff member may become an authority on sea cruises, another may work on trips to the Far East, and a third may develop an extensive knowledge of either low-budget or luxury trips. In some cases, travel agents are employed by national or international firms and can draw upon very extensive resources.

As salespeople, travel agents must be able to motivate people to take advantage of their services. Travel agents study their customers' interests, learn where they have traveled, appraise their financial resources and available time, and present a selection of travel options. Customers are then able to choose how and where they want to travel with a minimum of effort.

Travel agents consult a variety of published and computer-based sources for information on air transportation departure and arrival times, airfares, and hotel ratings and accommodations. They often base their recommendations on their own travel experiences or those of colleagues or clients. Travel agents may visit hotels, resorts, and restaurants to rate their comfort, cleanliness, and quality of food and service.

As travel consultants, agents give their clients suggestions regarding travel plans and itineraries, information on transportation alternatives, and advice on the available accommodations and rates of hotels and motels. They also explain and help with passport and visa regulations, foreign currency and exchange, climate and wardrobe, health requirements, customs regulations, baggage and accident insurance, traveler's checks or letters of credit, car rentals, tourist attractions, and welcome or escort services.

Many travel agents only sell tours that are developed by other organizations. The most skilled agents, however, often organize tours on a wholesale basis. This involves developing an itinerary, contracting a knowledgeable person to lead the tour, making tentative reservations for transportation, hotels, and side trips, publicizing the tour through descriptive brochures, advertisements, and other travel agents, scheduling reservations, and handling last-minute problems. Sometimes tours are arranged at the specific request of a group or to meet a client's particular needs.

In addition to other duties, travel agents may serve as *tour guides,* leading trips ranging from one week to six months to locations around the world. Agents often find tour leadership a useful way to gain personal travel experience. It also gives them the chance to become thoroughly acquainted with the people in the tour group, who may then use the agent to arrange future trips or recommend the agent to friends and relatives. Tour leaders are usually reimbursed for all their expenses or receive complimentary transportation and lodging. Most travel agents, however, arrange for someone to cover for them at work during their absence, which may make tour leadership prohibitive for self-employed agents.

Agents serve as bookkeepers to handle the complex pattern of transportation and hotel reservations that each trip entails. They

Facts About Travel Agents

- In 2008, travel agents booked 85 percent of all cruises, 70 percent of all tours and packages, 50 percent of all airline tickets, 30 percent of all hotels, and 25 percent of all vehicle rentals.

- Approximately 95 percent of travel agents use the Internet to conduct research or book travel for clients.

- Young people are more apt to use the services of travel agents than those age 55 and older. Forty-three percent of people who use the services of travel agents are between the ages of 35 and 54. Thirty-three percent are between the ages of 18 and 34.

- Ninety-three percent of travel agents charge a fee for their services—an increase of 29 percent since 1998.

Source: American Society of Travel Agents

work directly with airline, steamship, railroad, bus, and car rental companies. They make direct contact with hotels and sightseeing organizations or work indirectly through a receptive operator in the city involved. These arrangements require a great deal of accuracy because mistakes could result in a client being left stranded in a foreign or remote area. After reservations are made, agents write up or obtain tickets, write out itineraries, and send out bills for the reservations involved. They also send out confirmations to airlines, hotels, and other companies.

Travel agents must promote their services. They present slides or movies to social and special interest groups, arrange advertising displays, and suggest company-sponsored trips to business managers. They might also have a Web site that promotes their services.

REQUIREMENTS

High School
A high school diploma is the minimum requirement for becoming a travel agent. If you are interested in pursuing a career as an agent, be certain to include some computer courses, as well as typing or keyboarding courses, in your class schedule. Since much of your work as a travel agent will involve computerized reservation systems, it is important to have basic keyboarding skills and to be comfortable working with computers.

Because being able to communicate clearly with clients is central to this job, any high school course that enhances communication skills, such as English or speech, is a good choice. Proficiency in a foreign language, while not a requirement, might be helpful in many cases, such as when you are working with international travelers. Finally, geography, social studies, and business mathematics are classes that may also help prepare you for various aspects of the travel agent's work.

You can also begin learning about being a travel agent while still in high school by getting a summer or part-time job in travel and tourism. If finding a part-time or summer job in a travel agency proves impossible, you might consider looking for a job as a reservation agent for an airline, rental car agency, or hotel.

Postsecondary Training

Currently, most travel agencies do not require their agents to have college degrees. Increasingly, travel agencies are seeking applicants with college degrees, and when it comes to advancement, the agent with more education is likely to have an edge over those with less. Some colleges offer two- and four-year degrees in travel and tourism. If your college of choice does not offer a specific degree in travel and tourism, a degree in geography, communications, computer science, history, business, or foreign languages might be equally helpful. Other good college courses to take include computer science, world history, and accounting. The ASTA provides a list of member schools at its Web site, http://www.asta.org.

Another option for prospective travel agents is to take a short-term course in travel specifically designed to prepare you for work in this field. Such courses are typically between six and 18 weeks in length and are offered by community colleges, vocational schools, and adult education programs. The ASTA offers virtual seminars on industry-related topics, and there are a number of travel schools that combine home study with on-site training to prepare future agents. The Travel Institute is also a major provider of educational programs for travel professionals. It offers travel agents a number of other programs such as sales skills development courses, and destination specialist courses, which provide a detailed knowledge of various geographic regions of the world.

Certification or Licensing

To be able to sell passage on various types of transportation, you must be approved by the conferences of carriers involved. These are the Airlines Reporting Corporation, the International Air Transport

Association, and Cruise Lines International Association. To sell tickets for these individual conferences, you must be clearly established in the travel business and have a good personal and business background. Not all travel agents are authorized to sell passage by all of the above conferences. Naturally, if you wish to sell the widest range of services, you should seek affiliation with all three.

Travel agents may choose to become certified by The Travel Institute. The institute offers the designations of certified travel associate, certified travel counselor, and certified travel industry executive to applicants who complete education and experience requirements. While not a requirement, certification by the institute will help you progress in your career.

The Travel Institute also offers travel agents a number of other programs such as sales skills development courses and destination specialist courses, which provide a detailed knowledge of various geographic regions of the world.

The National Business Travel Association offers three types of designations for corporate travel professionals—corporate travel expert, certified corporate travel executive, and global leadership professional.

Most states do not require travel agents to be licensed or registered. However, there are exceptions, so it is important to check the requirements for the state in which you will be working.

Other Requirements

The primary requisite for success in the travel field is a sincere interest in travel. Your knowledge of and travel experiences with major tourist centers, various hotels, and local customs and points of interest make you a more effective and convincing source of assistance. Yet the work of travel agents is not one long vacation. They operate in a highly competitive industry.

As a travel agent, you must be able to make quick and accurate use of transportation schedules and tariffs. You must be able to handle addition and subtraction quickly. Almost all agents make use of computers to get the very latest information on rates and schedules and to make reservations.

You will work with a wide range of personalities as a travel agent, so skills in psychology and diplomacy will be important for you to have. You must also be able to generate enthusiasm among your customers and be resourceful in solving any problems that might arise. A knowledge of foreign languages is useful because many customers come from other countries, and you will be in frequent contact with foreign hotels and travel agencies.

EXPLORING

Any type of part-time experience with a travel agency will be helpful if you're interested in pursuing this career. A small agency may welcome help during peak travel seasons or when an agent is away from the office. If your high school or college arranges career conferences, you may be able to invite a speaker from the travel industry. Visits to local travel agencies will also provide you with helpful information.

If you are already pursuing a travel or hospitality career in college, you might also consider joining the Future Travel Professionals Club, organized by the ASTA. Membership allows you to network with professional members of the ASTA, attend chapter meetings, be eligible for scholarships, and receive an e-newsletter. For more information contact the ASTA (see sources at the end of this article).

EMPLOYERS

There are about 105,000 travel agents employed in the United States. Agents may work for commercial travel agents, work in the corporate travel department of a large company, or be self-employed (approximately 17 percent of workers). Travel agencies employ approximately two-thirds of salaried agents.

In addition to the regular travel business, a number of travel jobs are available with oil companies, automobile clubs, and transportation companies. Some jobs in travel are on the staffs of state and local governments seeking to encourage tourism.

STARTING OUT

As you start searching for a career in the travel field, you may begin by working for a company involved with transportation and tourism. Fortunately, a number of positions exist that are particularly appropriate if you are young and have limited work experience. Airlines, for example, hire flight attendants, reservation agents, and ticket clerks. Railroads and cruise line companies also have clerical positions; the rise in their popularity in recent years has resulted in more job opportunities. Those with travel experience may secure positions as tour guides. Organizations and companies with extensive travel operations may hire employees whose main responsibility is making travel arrangements.

Since travel agencies tend to have relatively small staffs, most openings are filled as a result of direct application and personal contact. While evaluating the merits of various travel agencies, you may wish to note whether the agency's owner belongs to the ASTA. This trade group may also help in several other ways. It offers online and home-study travel agent specialty courses. Also available, for members, is a travel agency management kit containing information that is particularly helpful to if you are considering setting up your own agency. Jobs are also listed on the Web sites of professional associations, including the ASTA Web site.

ADVANCEMENT

Advancement opportunities within the travel field are limited to growth in terms of business volume or extent of specialization. Successful agents, for example, may hire additional employees or set up branch offices. Experienced and skilled agents may advance to the position of *travel office* or *agency manager.* These managers are usually responsible for overseeing other travel agents, generating various reports, keeping track of finances, and generally managing all the activities of the travel agency.

A travel agency worker who has held his or her position for a while may be promoted to become a *travel assistant.* Travel assistants are responsible for answering general questions about transportation, providing current costs of hotel accommodations, and providing other valid information.

Travel agents may also advance to work as a *corporate travel manager.* Corporate travel managers work for companies, not travel agencies. They book all business travel for a company's employees.

Travel bureau employees may decide to go into business for themselves. Agents may show their professional status by belonging to the ASTA.

EARNINGS

Travel agents typically earn a straight salary. Although less common, some agents are paid a salary plus commission or work entirely on a commission basis. Salaries of travel agents ranged from less than $18,770 to $47,860 or more in 2008, with an average of $30,570, according to the U.S. Department of Labor. Managers with 10 years of experience may earn more than $65,000 annually. In addition to experience level, the location of the firm is also a factor in how much travel agents earn. Agents working in larger metropolitan areas tend to earn more than their counterparts in smaller cities. The ASTA offers a salary research tool at its Web site; users can search for salary information based on their experience level, state, agency size, and other criteria.

In the past, a significant portion of travel agency income came from commissions paid by airlines, hotels, car rental companies, cruise lines, and tour operators. In 2002, many large airlines stopped paying these commissions—except to preferred suppliers who brought large amounts of revenue to the airlines. To offset revenue losses from the elimination of commissions, more than 96 percent of travel agents now charge customers a fee for their services, according to the ASTA. The average fee for booking a flight was $36.79 in 2009. Some agents also charge for booking train travel, car rental, or hotels.

Most travel agency employers offer their employees health insurance, while approximately half offer life insurance and a dental plan. Small travel agencies provide a smaller than average number of fringe benefits such as retirement, medical, and life insurance plans. Self-employed agents tend to earn more than those who work for others, although the business risk is greater.

Those who own their own businesses may experience large fluctuations in income because the travel business is extremely sensitive to swings in the economy.

One of the benefits of working as a travel agent is the chance to travel at a discounted price. Major airlines offer special agent fares, which are often only 25 percent of regular cost. Hotels, car rental companies, cruise lines, and tour operators also offer reduced rates for travel agents. Agents also get the opportunity to take free or low-cost group tours sponsored by transportation carriers, tour operators, and cruise lines. These trips, called "fam" trips, are designed to familiarize agents with locations and accommodations so that agents can better market them to their clients.

WORK ENVIRONMENT

While this is an interesting and appealing occupation, the job of the travel agent is not as simple or glamorous as might be expected. Travel is a highly competitive field. Since almost every travel agent can offer the client the same service, agents must depend on repeat customers for much of their business. Their reliability, courtesy, and effectiveness in past transactions will determine whether they will get repeat business.

Travel agents also work in an atmosphere of keen competition for referrals. They must resist direct pressure or indirect pressure from travel-related companies that have provided favors in the past (free trips, for example) and book all trips based only on the best interests of clients.

Most agents work a 40-hour week, although this frequently includes working a half-day on Saturday or an occasional evening.

During busy seasons (typically from January through June), overtime may be necessary. Agents may receive additional salary for this work or be given compensatory time off.

As they gain experience, agents become more effective. One study revealed that 98 percent of all agents had more than three years' experience in some form of the travel field. Almost half had 20 years or more in this area.

OUTLOOK

The U.S. Department of Labor predicts that travel agents should experience little or no change in employment opportunities through 2018, with those who specialize in a travel destination, type of traveler, or mode of transportation expected to have the best opportunities. There are some factors, however, that may negatively influence the growth of jobs for travel agents. Many airlines and other travel suppliers now offer consumers the option of making their own travel arrangements through online reservation services, readily accessible through the Internet. There also are many Web sites that help travelers research, plan, and book trips. With these options, travelers have become less dependent upon agents to make travel arrangements for them. The travel industry is sensitive to economic changes and political crises that may cause international travel plans to be postponed. Therefore, the number of job opportunities for agents may fluctuate, depending upon the general political and economic climate.

Despite these negative factors, there will still be demand for travel agents. The public will still rely on them to help plan complex trips and suggest new or offbeat excursions or destinations. Travel agents with advanced educations and who specialize in a particular location, traveler demographic, or other travel area will have the best employment opportunities.

FOR MORE INFORMATION

Visit the society's Web site to read the online pamphlet Becoming a Travel Agent.

American Society of Travel Agents
1101 King Street, Suite 200
Alexandria, VA 22314-2963
Tel: 703-739-2782
E-mail: askasta@asta.org
http://www.astanet.com

This organization represents independent contractors, cruise and tour oriented agents, outside sales agents, and group oriented travel professionals. It is affiliated with the American Society of Travel Agents.

National Association of Career Travel Agents
1101 King Street, Suite 200
Alexandria, VA 22314-2963
Tel: 877-226-2282
E-mail: nacta@nacta.com
http://www.nacta.com

This organization represents travel managers and executives who seek to "balance employee needs with corporate goals, financial and otherwise." Visit its Web site for job listings, information on certification, and statistics on business travel.

National Business Travel Association
110 North Royal Street, 4th Floor
Alexandria, VA 22314-3234
Tel: 703-684-0836
E-mail: info@nbta.org
http://www.nbta.org

For information on travel careers in the U.S. government, contact
Society of Government Travel Professionals
4938 Hampden Lane, #332
Bethesda, MD 20814-2914
Tel: 202-363-7487
http://www.sgtp.org

For information regarding the travel industry and certification, contact
The Travel Institute
148 Linden Street, Suite 305
Wellesley, MA 02482-7900
Tel: 800-542-4282
E-mail: info@thetravelinstitute.com
http://www.thetravelinstitute.com

Index

Entries and page numbers in **bold** indicate major treatment of a topic.

A

Accreditation Board for Engineering and Technology Inc. (ABET) 14, 19, 24, 94
aerial applicators 28
aeronautical and aerospace technicians 5–15
  advancement 12
  certification/licensing 10
  earnings 12
  employers 11
  exploring 10–11
  high school requirements 9
  history 5–6
  job, described 6–9
  outlook 13–14
  overview 5
  postsecondary training 9–10
  requirements 9–10
  starting out 12
  work environment 13
aerospace engineers 16–27
  advancement 22
  certification/licensing 20
  Jennifer Dandrea interview 26–27
  earnings 23
  employers 21
  exploring 20–21
  high school requirements 19
  history 16–17
  job, described 17–19
  outlook 24
  overview 16
  postsecondary training 19–20
  requirements 19–20
  starting out 21–22
  work environment 23
Aerospace Industries Association of America (AIA) 10, 14, 24, 94
Aerospace Industries Association of Canada 15, 95
aerospace physiological technicians 7
aerospace technicians and technologists 6
agency managers 180
ag pilots 28
agricultural pilots 28–35
  advancement 33–34
  certification/licensing 31–32
  earnings 34
  employers 33
  exploring 32–33
  high school requirements 31
  history 28–29
  job, described 29–30
  outlook 34
  overview 28
  postsecondary training 31
  requirements 31–32
  starting out 33
  work environment 34

agriculture specialists 98
AHS International–The Vertical Flight Society 136
air battle managers 145
air carrier avionics inspectors 81
air carrier maintenance inspectors 81
air carrier operations inspectors 81
Air Combat USA 150
aircraft fuelers 127
aircraft launch and recovery technicians 7
aircraft mechanics 36–44
  advancement 42
  certification/licensing 40
  earnings 42
  employers 41
  exploring 41
  high school requirements 39
  history 36–37
  job, described 37–39
  outlook 43–44
  overview 36
  postsecondary training 39–40
  requirements 39–40
  starting out 41–42
  work environment 43
aircraft power plant mechanics 38
aircraft servicers 127
Air Force, U.S. 144, 151
Air Force Test Pilot School 151
airframe mechanics 38
air freight agents 126
airlift pilots and navigators 145
airline dispatchers 45–51
  advancement 50
  certification/licensing 48
  earnings 50
  employers 49
  exploring 49
  high school requirements 47–48
  history 45–46
  job, described 46–47
  outlook 51
  overview 45
  postsecondary training 48
  requirements 47–49
  starting out 49
  work environment 50–51
Airline Dispatchers Federation 45, 49, 51
Air Line Pilots Association, International 150, 161
airline reservation agents 168
Airlines Reporting Corporation 177
airline ticket agents 168
air marshals 52
airport concession workers 60
airport drivers 60
airport food concession attendants 60
airport food service workers 60
airport information specialists 61
airport janitors or cleaners 61